BEING

Awake, aware, and experiencing life
as your authentic self

Lynn B. Mann

First Edition

Text © Lynn B. Mann 2020

The moral rights of the author have been asserted.

A catalogue record for this book is available from the British Library.

ISBN: 978-1-8381628-3-2

Published by Being Books

Typesetting by Raspberry Creative Type, Edinburgh
Printed and bound by Totem

www.lynnbmann.com

For Stephen, who helped me find the start of my path to Being and walked with me along it for a while.

For Mick, who's untimely death robbed the world of a beautiful creative spirit and spurred me to finally put my writing out into the world, in case tomorrow never came.

Contents

Introduction

A Soul Imperative

The Quest to Fulfil Your Unique Potential as a Human Being

For as long as I can remember in my adult life, I've felt a drive, a compulsion, to understand *how to fulfil my unique potential as a human being*. Not in chasing symbols of success – a thriving career, marriage, children, or material possessions – more of an inner, visceral, soul imperative, to know, and be, who I truly am. This need has pulled me forward and helped me develop as a person, but also tormented me in equal measure. Sometimes it's felt like a blessing, sometimes a curse. It's been a need, a longing, to change and to grow – emotionally, psychologically, and spiritually. I don't think I'm alone in this search. I think many of us seek self-understanding and want to function better in the world – be happier, more fulfilled, and have a sense of purpose. To know who we really are, what we are meant to be doing with our lives, and to find some meaning to it all.

Over the past twenty years, I've trained and worked as a counsellor and therapist, read hundreds of books on psychology, self-development, and spirituality, watched and listened to hours and hours of videos, CDs, and podcasts, and written, and written, and written it all out. Like most of us, my efforts to change were often of the two-steps-forwards-three-steps-back variety.[1] Over time though, I realised I was learning the same lessons over and over again. I saw a common thread in all the concepts, theories, and philosophies, married with my own experiences of trial and error. I came to see that the thread that ran through everything, which pulled it all together, was all that was needed in itself. Everything else was helpful but not necessary.

All the time I felt the burning desire to understand who I truly was, this drive, this hunger, *is* who I truly am. All my reading, research and studying, all my soul-searching, finally brought me back to the drive itself, to my self, to my soul – and to Being. That very impulse to change, to fulfil our potential, to create, is actually Being itself. It's the spiritual Being that we are, existing in entanglement with the physical Being that we are.

<blockquote>
Being is what being human is really about.
Not the surface stuff. Not who we are in the world,
on the outside, or all the labels and roles, or our
history. Being is the lifeforce[2] within us.
</blockquote>

---

1   You can read more about my journey by turning to About the Author at the end of the book.
2   For the rest of this book I use the term 'lifeforce', which for me best describes what might also be called by other names: God, the Universe, Universal Energy, Source, Spirit, etc.

Escape into Being

I've always loved the quote by Pierre Teilhard de Chardin: 'We are not human beings having a spiritual experience, we are spiritual beings having a human experience.' This says it all for me. Anyone can conceptualise coming into Being, but we only come to know the truth of it by *experiencing* it, by living in it. When you create the space for Being to grow within you, connect with it, cultivate the connection, and allow it to guide you in creating all that you want your life to be, you'll realise it for yourself. One of the most fundamental benefits of doing this is that you get to escape into Being.

In our society, there is currently an obsession with 'chilling out'. Online, on social media, onscreen, and all around there seems to be a preoccupation with discussing and planning how to switch off, as an antidote to the pace and intensity of modern life. We want instant relaxation, or we just want to do nothing – hoping that hitting the pause button on life will help us cope better with its demands. Usually, this escape into instant relaxation is assisted by the soporific effects of excess, or a particular type of food and/or alcohol, or, for some, drugs. It doesn't really matter which decompression route you choose, you're more or less guaranteed temporary relief from the pace and intensity, or pain and problems, of your day-to-day existence, by the combined effect of the situation and consumable of choice.

So *why* aren't we all more relaxed, peaceful, and calmer? With all this time spent chasing nirvana, you'd think we'd be a society of super-chilled people with our lives in balance. Instead, we seem to be more stressed, more unhappy, more addicted than ever. Then, as if it's just that these escapes aren't good enough, or aren't working, we try for more and more of it, which still doesn't work. Or we want more intense experiences – spas, retreats, pilgrimages. We hope we'll find peace in certain places, or doing certain activities – meditation, yoga, or tai chi – and often end up thinking these are our only escape routes.

Often, when we're in these places, or doing these activities we find it even harder to silence our thoughts, relax, and switch off. Even when we have the ideal external conditions of tranquillity, silence, and solitude, we usually don't know how to truly relax and just Be. That is unless we've already developed the capacity to be on our own, find our Being, and be comfortable with it. We find it hard to be at peace because we haven't accessed the still and quiet within us. Our inside world doesn't match the outside one.

That's why you need to: *understand, recognise,* and *learn to experience,* living in Being. Then, you will find real rest and relaxation. You'll develop *deep peace and calm,* that you can turn to when you need to switch off from the world. It won't require planning, or be dependent on any situation, group of people, activity, or quantity of a particular food and/or alcohol. Instead, it will be entirely in your hands and available almost instantly.

Of course, you can still enjoy the chill-out times with food and/or alcohol as well, but the difference is you won't *need* them. Your rest and relaxation will also be more consistent and solid. You'll be nourished and nurtured by your rest and relaxation time, which is transformative in every area of your life.

*Ultimately, by learning to live in Being,
you will create a life you don't need to escape from.
Trust in the process, and it all just works beautifully.*

However, this is just the start of all that experiencing Being brings. As well as living *in* Being and coming to find an inner place of peace and calm, you can also come to live *from* Being. In doing this, you'll find your own voice, and a sense of empowerment to use it. Being seen and heard as your authentic self leads to a greater agency in your life, so you can bring your authentic power into the world, unapologetically.

Living from Being means experiencing a broader, richer version of your life than you have previously. Instead of being bombarded by the ever-changing contents of your mind, you'll have a more real and immediate connection to what is going on within you, and in your world. In time, you'll come to think and do from Being, which will transform your life. You'll live life more fully, as every day you'll become who you are meant to be. I know this is true because this has been my experience.

The Rollercoaster

For years and years, I lived on an emotional and psychological rollercoaster, caught in the thrall of my own mind, with all the compulsions, destructive behaviour patterns, and mental and emotional struggles, that went with it. I managed to function and have a façade of 'normality', and even 'success', but at a considerable cost. Any peace I experienced, usually via escape into food or alcohol, was short-lived and only compounded my problems, and generated additional psychological torture and emotional pain.

I knew how to pretend to be happy, but I wasn't. I knew how to get myself together enough to function in the world, even when I was screaming in my head and crying in my heart. I knew how to do what I needed to do to still be enough of the mother, daughter, wife, etc. that I wanted to be, whatever the cost, but emotionally, psychologically, and spiritually, I limped towards the times in between that I could retreat within to try to 'sort myself out'. I'd then spend a lot of time and energy trying to find a way to get back on track again or, at least, just try not to be in such a painful, self-destructive place.

Yet now, and for the past few years, as I've come to live more and more from Being, I feel like a different person. I rarely get over-stressed. I'm kinder to myself and others and no longer shred myself in my own mind as I used to. I feel grounded, often experiencing the holy grail of *a sense of equilibrium*, that I craved for years. More powerfully, though, I feel I know myself and that more and more I can be myself in my interactions. I connect with my own soul and express my true self more often than not now. I feel that I inhabit my Being, that I know my own voice, and feel empowered to use it to create all that I want to create in my life, and in the world.

I often can't believe that I've managed to get from A to B and turn things around. Actually, it feels like I've gone from A to Z! I thought I was a hopeless case, and life would likely never be any different. I feel so fortunate that I now get to experience life as my true self and from my soul. I remind myself of it daily. I also used to have the underlying feeling that there was really something *wrong* with me, that I needed to fix, so I could be more 'normal'. To not feel such a discrepancy between who I was on the outside, and felt I was on the inside. It's only now I can see that far from being something wrong with me in pursuing my authentic self, it was the best and healthiest thing I could do for myself. It's the growth impulse, and it's led me to precisely the right things to help me become who I truly am.

My hope in writing this book is that my experiences and realisations will resonate with you, and support you on your own journey from A to Z. I'll map out the process I went through, and have included some extracts from my journals, as I wrestled with psychological, emotional and spiritual questions. I believe that our human longing for connection is because of the need to share our spiritual journeys. We're meant to learn from each other and support each other in fulfilling the promise of our unique potential as human beings.

The Route to Being: Using this Book

In the following chapters, you'll discover the route to Being. To start, I'll explore what **Being** is and what you can hope to experience in your life through cultivating living *in* and *from* it. Then we'll delve into where most of us start, in **Head Stuff**: who we *think* we are; who we've been conditioned into thinking we are: by our upbringing, life experiences, and influences, our biology, as well as all the should and shouldn't rules we've absorbed. Living in our head detaches us from Being, and is the root of many of our psychological and emotional challenges.

In Part I, you begin to move into Being by shifting from **Head Stuff** to **Heart Stuff**. Here, you'll learn how to live more from your heart.

In Part II, we'll explore how to cultivate **The Five States of Being – Love, Awareness, Acceptance, Gratitude, Creativity** – that lead to **Transformation**. For each of the five states, I include **Key Points** and **Putting it into Practice** with tips and ideas to start cultivating each state within you. If you have been living mostly in your head until now, then the five states will work together to help you redress the balance. Ultimately, you are then able to start thinking and doing from Being. You inhabit Being. You become your integrated, whole self. This is not a complicated process, but it does take practice and perseverance. Your autopilot has most likely had you almost exclusively living in your head until now, so you need to *learn* to live from Being, but I can't stress enough how much it is worth it.

Part III is about **Transformation** because I sincerely believe if you want to create change in yourself and your life, then by the time you get to this stage of the book, you'll have all the information and inspiration you need to do it. In this section, you'll be ready to create a vision of how you want your life to be, and I share mine. We'll also look at some tools and practical building blocks that you can adapt to suit you, and which you'll slot into a transformation framework for yourself. I've included my own framework document, to show you all the elements of it, and how I adapted it through trial and error.

Throughout the book, you'll find references to a few of the books that I found helpful on my journey. You might also like to keep a notebook nearby as you work through the book, to write down some of the things that come up for you, and to take notes; it will help in creating your own **Vision and Framework** later on. Step by step, I'll take you through the process that brings you to know and be your true self, living the life you want to live.

* * *

You may find, as I did, that at times you feel inspired and see the picture of your life coming together piece by piece, only to at other times feel lost, alone, confused, or bereft of any understanding. I've learned lessons in various ways at different times and often thought that I had found the solution. It became apparent to me that there is no one 'answer', or 'key'. There is a collection of ways in which you can grow and change, which will lead you to come into Being. It's about trial and error to see what works for you, and about listening to your own wisdom. It's not about having to change your whole life, although maybe you want that. More likely, is that as you learn to live from Being, your life will change, for the better.

I wish you lots of love and luck and my dearest wish would be that you can come into Being more and more, enjoy the experience of it, and come to know and live from your true self. Most of all, I hope that you might begin to feel that you too are fulfilling the promise of your unique potential as a human being. I want to help you create that for yourself, whatever the life you would love to live looks like. There's no reason why you can't. I'm a testament to that. I'm just an ordinary human being the same as you, and I know that if I can transform my life, so can you.

PART I

Head to Heart: Uncovering Being

Chapter One

Being

*Being is where your soul resides -
your mortal, physical self and the
spiritual being that you are connect to
the infinite spiritual energy of the
lifeforce, and you draw it through you
into the world by directly experiencing it.*

What is Being? For me, the closest definitions relate to our essence, or nature, or living spirit. Being is our spiritual essence. It's our true nature, the core of who we really are. When we come into Being, we experience our true nature and connect with the energy of life, the lifeforce.

The problem with trying to define Being is that any names or labels immediately limit it, try to make it a static thing, and make it the same for everyone. In contradiction, Being is dynamic. It is flowing and ever-changing but also constant. Our awareness of it may fluctuate, but it doesn't change. It's there waiting for us to come back to it whenever we want.

The key word is *experiencing* because Being isn't just a concept or a state, we have to strive to maintain; it is experiencing the here and now, as it is, in this present moment. It is also the experience of recognising yourself as a spiritual Being, and it is experiencing, connecting with, and living from, your own soul. I've learned that the more fully I experience each moment, the more I live in Being; from there peace, happiness and equilibrium flow. Then the more fully that I'm connecting with and living from my soul, the more I'm bringing my unique Being into the world.

Recognising Being

Being is what experiences our thoughts and feelings. It took me a while to really understand that. To realise that there was a me noticing my thoughts, so I couldn't *be* my thoughts if I was noticing them. I could also observe how I was feeling, as well as experiencing it, so there must be a me that wasn't the feelings but observing them. This me, had to be something else, had to be separate from my thoughts and feelings, to be able to observe them.

To experience this for yourself, take a deep in-breath and breathe out slowly. Do this several times. Really concentrate on noticing your breathing. Then, at the end of an out-breath, pause, be still and notice the next thought that comes. Wait for it. Watch for it. At that moment, as you await the next thought, you are the observer of your mind; you are not *in* your mind, you are out of it, watching what thought will come next. You are resting in Being, you are experiencing Being. You are not experiencing living in your head, you are observing the contents of your mind, from Being, because they are two separate things.

Obviously, you can't do that all the time, but by experiencing it, you'll begin to get glimpses of Being, to experience what it feels like so that you can recognise it. You can then begin to cultivate Being in different ways, and come back to that place more and more often, through different routes or states, so that you can find what works best for you. The more you learn to recognise it and experience the difference from living in your head, the more you will want to create space to experience Being in your life.

Experiencing Being

In the past, when I read about people living more spiritual lives, and all the amazing ways of living and Being they were creating for themselves, I was doubtful that I could ever experience much of this myself. I thought they must just be more spiritually 'evolved' than me, a particular type of individual, or just blessed with a stronger spiritual connection. As I devoured the words of people transforming their lives or knowledge and wisdom from people who seemed to have figured it all out, the most I hoped for was that I would be a bit less messed up, and be able to function better in the world. I hoped that my inside states might more come to match the façade that I presented to the world. That I'd be a bit happier, and more mentally and emotionally stable.

What I'm about to tell you may seem like an exaggeration, and previously, I wouldn't have believed it was a possibility, for me. Hand on heart though, I can now say that I have regularly experienced all of the below.

- Positive energy
- Peace
- Happiness/joy
- Inspiration

- Instinctive action
- Creative expression
- Satisfaction
- Contentment
- Calm
- Tranquillity
- Aliveness/vitality
- Flow
- Emotional equilibrium
- Intuition
- Self-compassion and compassion for others
- Feeling centred and grounded
- Gratitude
- Deeper life understanding
- Presence
- Connection to my soul
- Sense of expansion
- Openness to people and experiences
- Present-moment focus
- Feeling empowered
- Faith
- A knowing
- Progress, and a feeling of continuity

- A sense of alignment

- Grace

- Serendipity

- Acceptance of my thoughts and emotions

- Selective thinking

- Absence of thinking

I know it's a long list, and I think I've probably even left some things out! And yes, I feel them all to varying degrees of intensity, depth, and not continuously, but it still feels miraculous that all of this is part of my experience of life at all. Of course, I still have to work at cultivating Being every day, and keep bringing my awareness back to it, and finding more and more ways to come back to it, again and again.

The other thing that amazes me is that I experience the painful psychological and emotional states of living in my head much less often now, and not to the same degree. When I do, by remembering to stay in awareness, and see them for what they are, I tend to be able to deal with them more quickly, and easily, than before. I can usually come back to Being and observe what's going on within me. When I do this, and I'm honest with myself, whatever has generated them tends to dissipate. This would have been impossible in the past, but it's all part of what has come with living more and more from Being.

> Being feels like where we were meant to be living
> all along. It's how we become healthy,
> happy and sane.

Living in and from Being - The Inflow and the Outflow

Building the foundation of Being, from coming out of your head and into your heart, cultivating awareness and acceptance, and coming to recognise the place of Being within yourself, brings you to your own soul. It establishes a connection if it was missing and strengthens any existing one.

In discovering who you really are, you come to know your own soul. You come into your own. In accepting all that you are, as your authentic self, you come to live *in* Being. This is the *inflow* of Being. The second part of the spiritual journey is living *from* your soul, and taking all that you have discovered – and all the promptings of your own instincts – out into the world, expressing Being, and your soul, in all that you do. This is the *outflow* of Being, where the lifeforce flows through you and into how you live, into what you do, into your relationships, guiding you to be and create all that you are meant to in the world. As author Sarah Ban Breathnach said, in her most well-known book *Simple Abundance*:[3]

'The authentic self is the soul made visible.'

When you come to recognise and live from Being, you'll get to know your own soul. The voice of your soul speaks to you in your hunches, your instincts for what is right, or wrong, for you. In your urges for what direction you need to take, and the decisions that you need to make. Often, these might not make sense in your head but stir your soul,

---

3   Sarah Ban Breathnach, *Simple Abundance* (Warner Books USA, 1995)

and you just *know* how you need to be in certain situations, or in relationships. You know, in a deep part of yourself, what's the right thing to say or do, and what your real needs and wants are. This applies from the huge life events, down to the minute-by-minute choices that we make every day, which accumulate to shape our psychological, emotional, physical, and spiritual self, and therefore, our lives.

The more you live from Being and connect to your own soul, the stronger your soul and its voice become. The more you can sense it, hear it, and trust in it. You begin to let it guide you in creating the life you are meant to be living, and in becoming your true, authentic, real, self. You won't have to figure it all out in your head, you will know instinctively what to do or not do, and in a calm, clear way, without the stress and the drama. Or you'll sit with it until you know, in your soul, what you need to do or not do. This book is borne out of me living in, and then from, Being – from connecting with my soul and letting the lifeforce flow through me into the world. It's only from living in Being, and then starting to recognise the voice of my own soul, that I started writing this book, and knew what I needed and wanted to say. I knew in my soul that I needed to get focused and determined and apply myself to making this book a reality, after writing it in small bits for years. My head was all about why I didn't have the time and mental space to do it. That with business and family commitments, it would be best to leave it until another time. But the voice of my soul was stronger. I felt that it wasn't giving me the option to turn my back on it.

Being has also enabled me to stay out of my head long enough as I write, in all the many, many hours has taken me, and actually enjoy the process. Trusting in it, rather than have it be angst-ridden. The book you are reading is tangible evidence of the reality of what I'm telling you about.

So, as you can see, this isn't theory. I've experienced coming to know my own soul, and I want to help you do the same. You may have had glimpses before, or maybe already feel connected to your soul, but whatever stage you are at on your own soul journey, coming more and more to live from Being can only enhance where you already are. Building on, or strengthening, any connection you already have, enriches the relationship, allowing you to experience more of the riches that living from your soul brings. Being develops and grows and deepens in layers, as you learn to fully experience each of the five states of Being and strengthen your spiritual muscles.

Lifeforce in Action - Transformation

As I mentioned, whenever you reside in Being and connect with your soul, you also connect with the lifeforce that infuses everything. Whatever we choose to call this lifeforce, we recognise that these names are all just labels, our best way of getting a handle on the great mystery that we somehow *know* exists but nobody sees or really understands.

For me, lifeforce is the spiritual energy from which love, inspiration, creativity, growth, expansion, connection, and vitality come. So, when that is flowing into me, but I'm locked in my head and not connected to Being, there won't be much of a flow of spiritual energy through me, as I won't be drawing on it. Any that does flow into me is stagnant energy. On the other hand, when I come into Being, and I connect with that spiritual energy flowing into me, and draw on it, guess what? More flows in, and the more I pull on it, the stronger it flows.

> The lifeforce *wants* to flow into you, to fill you up
> with spiritual energy, for you to fully inhabit
> the spiritual Being that you are, and fulfil your
> unique potential as a human being –
> *by living in communion with it.*

So far, I've taken a stab at defining Being, looked at recognising it in ourselves, described what can come from experiencing it. The next natural step is to learn how to begin to live from that place. The more you live in Being, the more Being will start to flow out into your life, this is when you begin to live and love and create in the world *from* Being.

Shortly, we'll break Being down into building blocks, so you'll be able to start creating a foundation of Being from which to live your life. First, in the next chapter, we'll explore the opposite – what living in our heads brings us. To illustrate why you might want to cultivate Being.

KEY POINTS: BEING

- Being is your spiritual essence, your true nature.

- Being isn't a concept, it's an experience.

- Living in Being is what draws the lifeforce into your mortal, physical self.

- Your soul resides at this intersection, in Being.

- You can practise recognising Being within yourself and cultivate experiencing it.

- Huge rewards flow from coming to inhabit Being.

- First, you learn to live *in* Being, then to live *from* it.

- Through living from Being, the lifeforce flows through you, into the world, in all that you are and all you create.

Chapter Two

Head Stuff

It's all in your head!
You are more than the contents
of your mind.

Who are we in the world? How do we want to be perceived? What's the outer representation of ourselves that we've put a great deal of mental and emotional energy into maintaining? It's a collection of all the labels we give ourselves, and that society gives, or imposes on us: tall/short, thin/fat, healthy/unhealthy, employed/unemployed, rich/poor, etc. It is all the roles we fulfil: wife/husband/partner, mother/father/carer, daughter/son, or the type of work we do. It's also all the personality and character traits that we think most accurately define who we are: *I am*: kind, stubborn, determined, productive, aggressive, shy, friendly, confident, adventurous, nervous, and so on, and so on. Endlessly we categorise and pigeonhole ourselves, or have it done for us. We accept them, often even if we don't like them, or alternatively, fight them, and create defences against recognising, or owning, them.

Who we are in our heads is created out of all our life experiences from our first breath to right now reading these words. We never stop absorbing the influences around us:

the myriad experiences we've had through childhood, in our families and at school, with our friends, in society, in our careers, in all the rules we've taken on board, in all the influences we've soaked up. These experiences have shaped what we have become today, yet we were rarely conscious of the human being that we were becoming.

This version of us, however, only lives in our heads. It is not who we actually are. It is who we *think* we are. We've created the narrative of who we are in our minds since we were born, and just keep adding to it, or editing it, as we go through life. We take in all that we experience daily and interpret it whichever way best suits us to keep our stories evolving. Only adding to the narrative which serves us best, at any given time. That's all they are though, stories, our interpretation of events, with our perspective on them, and our selective memory.

Sometimes we might catch ourselves telling the 'story of me' to somebody else, or even to ourselves, and notice the embellishment, or the dramatisation, or the omissions. We recognise it's not really the whole truth of who we are. It is not reality, just a version of it. *Our* version of it. These stories are something that happened at a point in time and are gone, they are only kept alive in our heads, they are only part of who we are *in our heads*, not in reality.

> Our stories don't need to be part of who
> we are any more. Only if we allow them to be,
> by *thinking* that they are.

Your mind wants you to think that these stories are real though, that they are who you really are, that they are *all* that you are. It wants that because *your mind wants to be in control.* Your mind wants you to think that all these stories, all these labels, and roles, and personality traits, and characteristics, and habits, and behaviours, and compulsions, and fears, and the constant stream of thoughts, are who you really are. It wants this because it generates all the stories, all the ideas of who you are. It doesn't want you to see them for what they are, or get another perspective on them or, heaven forbid, let them go. It wants you to think that they are who you are because your mind wants you to believe that *it* is who you are. That all you are is the contents of your head, and it so it pulls you back into the stories, to *it*, to being locked in your mind, living your life in your head.

The Boss

Your mind wants to be the boss, and of course, biologically there is a sound evolutionary imperative for that. The brain is our control centre: it directs operations, keeps us breathing and able to eat, sleep, walk, drive, work, and all the multitude of activities we carry out on any given day automatically, without having to even give any of it a single thought. It is our incredible, awe-inspiring human-computer. It needs to run its programs and carry out its routines, it needs to be in charge of *everything,* and for efficiency, it wants to run the show *completely.*

However, because the mind has all its systems and processes in place, it tends to see anything and everything as a threat. So it's on alert, constantly scanning, assessing the impact of whatever is going on around about us, or within us, at any given time, and adjusting accordingly.

This is the start of the problem. Due to the sheer volume of what our minds take in, much of it new information, a lot of the time our minds perceive input as a threat when it isn't. This sets off a chain reaction of stress in the body, which can make us mentally or physically unwell. This state of alert has gone into overdrive, as the intensity and pace of our lives have increased dramatically over a few decades. Our poor minds haven't had time to evolve into an updated version, that might be more able to cope with the information overload of the ever-increasing quantities of data bombarding it, at a faster and faster speed, from an ever-expanding array of sources. There is rarely any time where it isn't on duty, called upon to understand things, figure things out, strategise, plan, remember, reflect, catalogue – all while still carrying out the automatic processes that we take for granted. Phew!

Our minds are overwhelmed and under pressure and, like any dictatorial boss, our mind wants us serving it, and doesn't want our attention wandering away anywhere else. Certainly not to our emotions, and especially not to the spiritual beings that we are – as that would undermine its authority. Any sniff of it and the mind pulls our full attention back towards it: we get anxious, we get scared, we ruminate over the same thoughts compulsively, we get depressed or angry, we get tense. We're back to being locked in our minds, going round and round in our heads, living there most of the time. Controlled by a boss that we've been so bullied by all our lives, that we just accept its dictates without question. We can only focus on dealing with the fallout from dancing to the tune of that boss as best we can.

It doesn't have to be this way, though. When you begin to see how much you are a slave to your own mind, and how much you live your life in your head, you also start to realise that it isn't actually you. It's part of you but not the essence of you. Crucially, you acknowledge that the mind is a part of you that you can have control *over* rather than be controlled *by*.

> How good will it feel when you hand in your notice to your mind dictator and become your own boss — psychologically, emotionally, and spiritually?

Becoming Your Own Boss

The fact is you can *choose* not to live in your head all the time. You can *choose* not to be at the mercy of your mind. You can *choose* to live more from your body, your instincts, your soul. By choosing to live from an emotional, then spiritual, place within you, you can withdraw from your mind at will, and come back to it at will, it's as easy as that. Well, nearly. Of course, you have to learn to do it.

We're never taught how to live outside of our heads, and really be in our bodies, comfortable with our emotions, discovering the spiritual Beings that we are; we have to cultivate the ability. The good news is that this ability is available to us all and can be learned. There is a clear process for doing it, which I'll outline for you in the next chapter.

Unfortunately, we're addicted to living in our heads. It's so ingrained in us, and endemic, and rewarded, in our culture, that we have grown up seeing that as the norm, never questioning it. It's mesmerising. You may even feel a little panic and fear at the prospect of not thinking so much.

The sense of being in control that living in our heads gives us, makes us feel more secure. It's false security though. We *feel* like we're in control, but we're not.

Recognising that you're living your life in your head is the beginning of the journey to freedom from the tyranny of it. You'll recognise how much you're living in your head by how tense or stressed you feel, how often your mind races, how often your thoughts are on future or past events, rather than on what is happening in the moment that you are in. If you are rarely aware of the breath going in and out of your lungs several times a minute, rarely feel a sense of peace and calm, and the absence of any thoughts, chances are, like most of the population, you're living in your head.

Maybe in you, it manifests more in your behaviour patterns, such as criticism, judgement, anger – either towards yourself, others, or both. These, in turn, lead to the next layer of consequences: headaches, sleeplessness, anxiety, or depression, and can result in physical, as well as psychological and emotional, ill health. Many chronic diseases are now known to be, if not directly caused by stress, then exacerbated by it. We also now know that many of these chronic illnesses can be slowed, and even reversed, in part, by dealing with the stress that comes from living in our minds.

For many of us, living in our heads becomes such an unhappy, unfulfilling, lonely, or tormented place to live, that it leads us to seek another place within ourselves to live from. Whatever your experience, knowing that it isn't working for you any more, is the first step. Even if it has taken you many painful experiences to come to that conclusion. When you recognise that you are *living in* your head, you no longer believe you *are* the contents of your head. You begin to take back control. You then work towards being able to choose where you live from in yourself.

Time and Energy

Living in our heads, thinking incessantly, planning, strategising, remembering past events, rehearsing conversations, jumping from one to the other, all day long, most days, keeps us locked into the space of using psychological energy. The problem is we spend most of our available life energy in psychological gymnastics. We get really good at directing our energy there and working out in that space. However stressful it may be, we are comfortable there, because it's what we know. After all, it's where we spend nearly all of our time.

Until some strong emotions bubble up, if we let them, or can't stop them, and then we have to redirect some of our energy into dealing with the emotional situation/ drama/crisis. This is probably a lot less comfortable than being in the psychological space, in our head, where we feel in control. Our emotions usually feel trickier to deal with, more unpredictable, volatile, and scary. Boy, can emotions also suck up our energy supplies. Therefore, we tend to react to the emergence of the emotional stuff by, for example, venting, denial, trying to escape, ignoring it, or trying to anaesthetise the discomfort of it in ourselves, with food, with alcohol, drugs, sex, shopping . . . whatever distraction works best for each of us. Temporarily we escape the emotions, and when they damp down enough, we can get back into our heads, where, however bad it gets in there, or whatever the repercussions, we're more used to it. Where we're more comfortable – relatively.

Most of us are uncomfortable with living in our emotional space for long, as we've never been taught how to. We're out of our comfort zone there.

Instead of *spending* our time and energy this way, we could instead *invest* it. Creating the life we want, by choosing where to put our attention, rather than being locked into autopilot – just letting our mind decide where our attention goes, like a runaway train.

Beginning to withdraw from living in your head means that your attention is not totally caught up in your mind. You have free psychological time to put your attention elsewhere. Your mind isn't soaking up all of your energy, so you have extra energy supplies. The really, really good news, however, is that when you start to live more and more from Being, that actually generates energy, rather than depleting it. So, not only are you gaining time and energy by withdrawing from the mind, you are generating more energy supplies through being nourished spiritually.

It's that simple. You get to choose in every moment of every day where you put your attention. What you want to spend your time and energy *experiencing*, and therefore, what you spend your life experiencing. Do you want to spend your time and energy experiencing all that living in your head brings, every day, with only escapes that come at a cost? Or do you want to spend your time, energy, and your life, experiencing the rewards of living more from Being?

Seems like a no-brainer to me – forgive the pun! Living from Being, you don't stop thinking – no lobotomy is needed. You still get to use your wonderful brain, and it will still be a runaway train sometimes. You will be much more the boss, though. You will have much more control and choice. You will have a different relationship with your own mind, and get it to work *with* you, rather than against you. It can then support you in becoming who you truly are and creating the life you want to live.

Knowing Your Mind

You may, as I did, still feel that the answer lies *in* your head. In exploring how your mind works and trying to figure out what is 'wrong' with it, or with you, that is causing you to suffer psychologically and emotionally. You may feel you just haven't quite got a grasp yet of how the ego operates, or discovered what particular psychological disorder you suffer from. You may believe if only you could find it, it would solve all your problems.

Don't waste your time and energy going down this road, or at the very least, do it at the same time as you learn to live more from Being. This is why.

After years of studying, researching, and reading psychology, neurology, and self-help books, I felt that I understood a lot more about how my brain worked, and what caused me to repeat self-destructive and addictive patterns. I realised why I self-sabotaged and had all these conflicting aspects of myself at odds with each other, and on and on and on. Even though these new discoveries or understandings helped for a short time, I always seemed to end up back in the same place, feeling the same way, as though I was back at square one. I felt that knowing how my mind was wired, and what was generating the self-destructive behaviours that created so much unhappiness for me was good to know, but it didn't bring any lasting change. *It wasn't changing my experience of life.* I began to realise that all of this was just keeping me in my head, so rather than solving the problem, it *was* the problem. Since being in my head was the problem, in time I realised that the real answer was to first *come out of my head.*

That's not to say there isn't value in learning about how the mind works, reading about the various theories and therapies, because there is massive value in exploring these materials. If you haven't already, it can be interesting and helpful, but don't seek *the answer* there. Come out of your head, and learn to live from Being, first. Then, if you still feel the need or the desire, or just the interest, to know more about how the mind works, and how you, in particular, might be wired, do it. It can be fascinating. At the end of this book, you'll find a list of fantastic books that I've enjoyed, or found helpful over the years.

Journal:
Living in Your Head – The Movie

Before we explore how to move towards a more heart-based experience of life, I'd like to share a few of my journal extracts from several years ago. The entries document the havoc caused by living entirely in my head: the almost daily psychological and emotional pain, the suffering, the turmoil, that I lived with – nearly all of it self-inflicted, through being locked in my mind. Of course, I didn't realise that at the time. I just thought there was something wrong with me. That even though I was reasonably intelligent, I was somehow psychologically and emotionally inadequate. That I was different, that I was damaged, that I hadn't been taught how to deal with my mind and emotions properly – assuming that others had!

Lost

I feel like I'm screaming in my head! I feel so far from where I was recently when I was beginning to feel calmer and more centred. I feel distressed. I feel lost – like I'm somewhere I don't know how to get out of. I keep trying to pick my way through the jumble of thoughts in my head like I'm stumbling through the rubble of a demolished building. There just seems to be too much to sort out just now, too many things going on, too much to think about. I feel overwhelmed with it all. I don't know where to start in trying to get a handle on just regrouping and moving forwards.

As I write this, I realise I'm locked in my mind. I'm completely lost in it and have been for hours, with absolutely no sense of my body, or where I am. As I note this and look out of the window to the garden, I slip out of my head into this room, and I can feel the grip of my mind on me lessening. I feel the residue of feeling like I was going mad, still lingering. I can feel the physical tension and tightness in my head, but I feel like I've come back to myself, and to reality.

As I take a deep breath, my chest feels tight, as if I haven't breathed for a while. Maybe I've only been breathing shallowly. I'm battling inside to keep out of my head, to not be seduced back by the thoughts that seem to be urgently demanding my attention, trying to pull me back from being aware. I'm battling to avoid being consumed by my mind again.

I don't understand why I have so quickly got to this extreme in my own head. Trying to understand though takes me back into my head, keeps the turmoil going. I need to just breathe and look out the window for a while and try not to think.

Blackness

Over the past few days, I've felt myself sinking into apathy and depression. I've been feeling it on and off for weeks now. I don't think it's actual depression, more a depressive state, a melancholy, an apathy, a sadness, and sometimes it feels overwhelming. It feels like the 'black fog' people talk about.

Sometimes there seems to be a cause, a catalyst, and sometimes it feels unrelated to anything. I get a feeling of 'What's the point?' A complete lack of motivation. I want to escape, I want to be alone, but I also don't want to do anything. I feel like I want to retreat from the world. It feels like a chore to interact with people. I don't want to have to speak. I want to sit and do nothing and stare at a wall.

Anxiety

I notice my mind buzzing with minutiae a lot of the time, over and over, minor detail after minor detail, flitting through my head. Most of the time, it's also attached to feeling anxious – planning, organising, checking, list-making. Why do I find myself rehearsing conversations that aren't even about anything important? What's the point of wasting all that mental energy? It's 99 per cent unnecessary and just creates tension in me and takes me away from now.

I have to become aware of what I do to foster, encourage, and perpetuate this state. I must feel, subconsciously, that I get some benefit from it to keep doing it. A sense of control? It's too much though, it's counter-productive and keeps me in my head.

My mind wants me to stay in my mind. It keeps me there by grabbing my attention with all the details of anything and everything. It doesn't want me to ignore it. That's what it feels like anyway.

Groundhog Day

No, no, no! I've ended up in this place again. Rocking on my bed at 1 a.m., not wanting to lie down because I'm dreading the migraine I know I'm likely to get. Feeling sick, bloated, and poisoned after several days of overindulgence in excess food, sugar, and alcohol. Just needing to write it all out, as a release, as a cry to myself for help. A plea to stop doing this to myself.

I feel so disappointed in myself and so frustrated. I had been eating so healthily, and doing yoga, and feeling good, and now I feel awful. Why, why, why do I do this to myself? I end up back at this same place over and over again, and I hate it. I hate myself for it.

It feels so painful in my head, physically and psychologically, and in my heart, and my soul. I know I'm going to be in so much turmoil for days trying to get myself back on track and dealing with how terrible I'm going to feel, physically, mentally, and emotionally.

Line in the sand time again. How many times am I going to draw a line then cross it again? How long will it take this time until I'm back here? That's depressing. What can I do to make this line in the sand not get washed away by the tides of life this time? Actually, by my own self-destructive behaviours.

Twirly Mind

Tension, tension, tension. Again, my mind is flitting about, and I am finding it hard to step back from engaging with it. I'm finding it hard to let go and reside in peace and the present.

What can help me become more at peace and more present?

- *Breathing in deeply, and out very slowly, with a pause between each breath, three to five times, or more.*

- *Lie on the floor and do some stretches.*

- *Be still and stare at the sky, garden, hills, or wall, and just notice my breathing as I do.*

- *Read something from One Minute Mindfulness.*[4]

- *Walk outdoors, taking in my surroundings.*

- *Write it all out, onto paper.*

- *Listen to a spiritual audio CD.*

- *Re-read some journal entries.*

Escape

Escape from what? What is it I want to escape from? When I drink alcohol and overeat, especially sugar, it feels like an escape. I think it's an escape from my own thoughts, or mental and/or physical tension in general, uncomfortable feelings, maybe boredom, frustration, inadequacy, fear ...

When I want to escape, I kind of go into a mode of being on a track that it's hard to derail myself from. I'm in my head, and I'm disconnected from my soul. I can't hear the desires of my soul, or very faintly, and not with enough impetus to stop me from following the desire of my head for escape. This takes me down the familiar roads of tired behaviour patterns, and responses that feel like the only option when I get to a certain point on the road.

Alcohol and excess sugar eventually (quite quickly) create in me a negative frame of mind, usually from feeling bad physically, and that then creates the desire for further escape

---

4   Simon Parke, *One Minute Mindfulness* (Hay House UK, 2014)

from the bad feelings – bad feelings created by the alcohol/ overeating/excess sugar in the first place.

Rather than bringing escape, they are the cause of the need to escape, they trigger the cycle. But my mind is generating these very things that it wants to escape from, it's all part of the perpetuation of the mental drama.

Behaviour Patterns

It seems clear to me today that my impulses and urges are mental rather than physical, but they trigger emotional states that make the impulses and urges feel like physical cravings. I'm then using physical ways (usually excess food/ sugar or alcohol) to manage these mentally and emotionally, and sometimes spiritually generated states.

How many times do I need to learn this same lesson?! Why am I still doing the same things that I've known for years only give me a temporary relief or distraction and actually make things worse? Why am I using my precious life energy and time in going round in these same circles over and over for years?

If my raison d'etre is to fulfil my unique potential as a human being, why do I spend so much time either in behaviours, or thought patterns, that at best distract me from pursuing this goal, and growing spiritually? At worst, they are destructive and actually take me backwards, undoing some of the progress, or expansion of my spirit, that I'd already achieved.

What's the answer? I feel like I need to find a spiritual response to the impulses, urges, and cravings, instead of trying to manage them in physical ways. I think I need to be aware of the mind patterns and emotions behind the impulses, urges, and cravings, instead of looking outwards for an answer to them. I need to seek the answers inwardly.

Towards Being

I realise I've been driving myself mad. I've been consumed by my mind. My diet has been off the rails, drinking alcohol too often, and not doing any exercise. I've been entirely in the thrall of my mind, my ego, satisfying its demands for more, and instant gratification, and escape – whatever it wants. I've been in intense emotional and psychological pain on and off for weeks, and I've been full of self-loathing and regret at how badly I've gone astray from sticking to my plans, and how awful it's left me feeling physically.

I've been beating myself up mentally and not wanting to see anyone or have to function for days, but have had to, and that has taken a gargantuan effort, and compounded the painful feelings.

Eventually, eventually, eventually, when I couldn't stand the content of my own mind any more, I remembered I just needed to come back to Being – to the here and now. I pulled my attention out of my head and directed it towards my breathing. I kept doing it over and over. I concentrated on whatever was simple and right in front of me. I focused on feeling in my body and the present – on doing things slowly. Soon I could feel myself calming emotionally and mentally. I felt more soothed and saner the more I did it.

I felt like I was clinging onto doing it. Like it was a life raft that would take me to the safety of peace and sanity, and it did. I got sane, I felt at peace, and I got back on track again, but next time I want to remember to come back to Being as soon as I start going off track in the first place.

In Part II, I talk about the five states of Being, the above experiences of living in my head are really the states of the head. The states that we can get into through living disconnected from Being. And boy, did I get myself in a state sometimes.

KEY POINTS: HEAD STUFF

- You are not the labels, roles, and identity that you present to the outside world.

- You are not your stories or your past.

- You live at the mercy of the dictatorial boss that is your own mind, and it wants to be completely in control.

- Becoming more aware of how your mind seeks to control you is the first step towards Being.

- Once you stop spending so much time and energy locked in your mind, you can invest in cultivating Being, and so generate more energy and spend less time thinking.

- You get to choose in every moment of every day where you put your attention, how you spend your time and energy, and therefore what you spend your life experiencing.

Chapter Three

Heart Stuff

The head/heart dichotomy is something that most of us wrestle with, usually unconsciously. We become more conscious of it within us, as we begin to cultivate Being. Choosing our heart over our head is central to living more from Being.

I hope that you can now see how experiencing Being is quite different from living in our heads. They can feel like night and day, like polar opposites, at odds with each other. I talked about our programming being located in our head, but when it comes to Being, it's much harder to sense its location. When I was first trying to live more and more in Being, I found it difficult to get a sense of where I was *going*, in trying to reside there more. Through cultivating awareness, I began to understand that although Being infuses our whole body, it is centred in our hearts, obviously not our actual, physical heart, but in our sense of where our emotional centre is, at our core.

Through conceptualising Being as residing in my heart, I felt more able to grasp that I was aiming to just choose between head stuff and heart stuff. I found it easier to come into Being by thinking of this concept of head/heart. By staying more connected to our hearts, we gradually come to feel more connected to Being. This became a shortcut to Being for me. We cannot switch off our minds, but we can choose where to put our attention. We can actively come out of our head, over and over and over, and aim to only go into our head when we are rooted in our heart, in Being.

As I described in Chapter 1, in modern society, we live mostly in our heads, consumed by the narrative of our lives, which wreaks havoc on us as spiritual beings. It leaves us sick in our souls, hurting, needing something, or just trying to escape from the pain. This pain and turmoil come from living in our heads and ignoring the prompting of our soul, where the answers lie. These nudges urge us to come to know what we want and don't want, and towards what will lead us to satisfaction, fulfilment, and happiness. Until we realise that these uncomfortable feelings, the pain, and turmoil within us, are being revealed by our most authentic self, our Being, we will continue to experience them. Being is showing us what staying locked in our head is creating for us, it is urging us to turn towards it instead and engage with it.

Which Me Do I Want to Be?

This is the question you have to ask yourself, in the moment, and continuously. In doing so, you make a choice whether to live in your head or your heart and therefore choose the life you experience. This is what I discovered as the differences between being totally Head Me or totally Heart Me – ring any bells?

Head Me

Thinking, thinking, thinking, organising, mentally re-iterating lists, internally criticising and judging myself and others, tension, resentments, rushing around, shoulders up, barely breathing, lost to the here and now and reality. Paying attention to every thought, every opinion, that pops into my head, every worry, every annoyance, every grievance. Resisting everything, and more or less continually wanting something else than *what is*. Then wanting to escape from the psychological pain of things not being the way I want them to be.

Head Me creates mental and emotional turmoil, physical tension, and pain. My head physically hurts with it. It often feels like some kind of torture to be in the grip of it. It generates feelings of stress, unhappiness, entitlement, depression, loneliness, resentment, isolation, aggression, alienation, and confusion to varying degrees at different times, depending on the circumstances and situation.

Head Me wants other people to be there or not be there when it suits me. It also wants them to be the way I want them to be, to do what I want them to do, and leave me alone when I want to be alone.

Head Me can't rest, it can only escape into alcohol, or a screen, or be sedated by food. Even then it's merely dormant, ready to pounce when the distraction of the escape is over, and usually more powerfully than before because it is never satisfied. Usually, when head me is happy, it is in a high, manic, overexcited, intense way that feels hard to contain. Sometimes I feel worn out by head me. I just want to switch off my head, to silence its constant barrage of output which it expects me to pay attention to.

In Head Me, my self-concept is of whichever labels, roles, or aspects of my personality or character are to the forefront of my mind at that time, due to the given situation or circumstances, or dependent on my state of mind, or interactions with others. Given all of that, my self-concept, when I'm fully Head Me, is an ever-changing, complicated kaleidoscope of contradictions!

> Head Me is completely self-absorbed,
> it can see nothing else but its own concerns and
> wants them front and centre stage at all times,
> consuming my attention and energy.

Heart Me

Heart Me is in my body, and in the here and now, and in reality. Heart Me is relaxed and open and looking to accept and understand things, and find solutions to things. It keeps things calm and looks for the best perspective on things. It doesn't want to create any dramas. When I'm in my heart and thinking, my thinking is much slower, more deliberate, reflective, and contemplative.

Heart Me feels more connected to others. I feel compassion for them in all their flawed humanity, as they are inherently the same as me. I'm more accepting, empathising with their struggles, and much less inclined to judge or criticise, and notice when I do. I try to treat others as I'd want to be treated if I were them, in their place. I don't beat myself up by judging and criticising myself either. I accept and have compassion for myself. I appreciate that I am just doing my best at any given time with who I am and where I am on my journey.

In Heart Me, I allow myself to just be who I am in truth and openness, without feeling I have to justify, excuse, or feel guilty about any of that. I'm just a human being, being human, flaws and all. I let myself Be. I go with the flow of life rather than try to shape life to suit me.

In Heart Me, my self-concept runs much deeper, is
less changeable, and more dependable.
It is of my human qualities as a compassionate,
loving, creative, and positive person,
living with an open heart.

The Switch from Head to Heart

Of course, we are rarely entirely Head Me or Heart Me. The two continuously co-exist, and how much we live in each depends on the choices we make, and where we put our attention. The majority of us tend to live as some version of Head Me to whatever degree, most of the time. So how do you switch from living most of your life as Head You to becoming more Heart You, and why would you want to anyway?

Think about all that you experience when you are Head You, and how that feels. My guess is it's often not much fun. It certainly wasn't for me. Yes, I got lots of stuff done, and kudos for having such a full, busy life. I *seemed to* manage to keep all the balls in the air so beautifully. However, the experience of it for me was quite different from how it looked on the outside. When your experience of living your life solely in your head isn't helping you to be the person you want to be, and create the life you want, then your only option is to do it differently. Start to explore who Heart You is, recognise it within yourself, and start to choose to live more from your heart.

Whatever is going on in your head, how do you want to feel, and what do you want to be experiencing? You get to choose. You get to choose to be more Head You or Heart You. In doing so, you decide how you live, moment by moment, day after day. Your head will *always* come up with good reasons for you to stay with it, to keep you thinking, keep you locked in your grievances, resentments, negativity, worries, plans etc. With every choice between head and heart, you decide whether you experience the intensity, tension, or emotional turmoil of Head You, or experience feeling relaxed, in touch with your emotional state, and aware of reality, as Heart You.

When you choose to live more from your heart, you don't stop thinking, but the incessant stream of thought slows down. It's less intense. You get a bit of distance from it. You become detached enough from your thoughts that you start to notice your thoughts, instead of just thinking them. You view them more objectively. Also, as you live less in your head, your mind slows down, and far fewer automatic, repetitive thoughts are generated.

Living in Integrity

In her brilliant book *Untamed*, author Glennon Doyle[5] says, 'Integrity means having one self. Ensuring that my

5   Glennon Doyle, *Untamed* (Random House, 2020)

inner and outer self are integrated.' When we're living in our head, as we looked at in Chapter 2, we think that we *are* all our labels and stories, and this is who we present to the world. In our heart, we know that there is another us. Our inner self, that we keep more, or almost wholly, hidden. Our suspicions and instincts for who we really are usually stay locked inside.

It's natural to have aspects of ourselves we keep more private, or just reveal to certain people. It's valid self-protection to only do that with people that we trust. It becomes less healthy though, when there are discrepancies between who we portray to the world, and who we feel we really are inside, or if we think we can't be our true selves with anybody. The more significant the difference, the more likely it is to affect us negatively – mentally, emotionally, and in our lives.

Even just acknowledging that we have two different selves – and exploring who the more hidden self is, and why we feel we need to keep it hidden – can lessen its negative impact. Often, even just being honest with yourself can be a relief, even if you don't feel ready to outwardly express your inner self yet. Paying attention to who you are on the inside and noticing who you present yourself to be in the world, you'll begin to discover which feels truer for you. Getting to really understand what moves and motivates you helps you become more comfortable with yourself. Then you're able to more objectively decide which aspects of that self you'd like to express more. Ultimately, over time, who you are on the inside can become who you are on the outside too. Then you're living as an integrated, authentic, whole person. You are just 'one self'. You are just yourself.

The more you come into your heart, and into Being, you'll understand yourself better, begin to know your authentic self, begin to trust in it, and feel more comfortable expressing that self in the world. Each step you take in this direction builds momentum over time, until you fully inhabit your whole, integrated self, in Being.

Inner strength and a sense of freedom come from being your authentic self.

Your head and your heart can work in harmony. They make a dynamic team. Much more powerful than living in your head alone, primarily disconnected from your heart. First, however, you'll have to swing the pendulum the other way, and really learn how to live from your heart, before you get the hang of being in your head while still connected to your heart.

Living from Your Heart

When you live from your heart, you are in Being and actively choosing to live from love. As you dwell there, by paying attention to your emotional core, you'll come to understand what is important to you, what your priorities are, and how you want to be in the world. As we'll look at, practising awareness and acceptance helps open us up to the expansiveness of love, and creates space for it to grow and infuse our whole Being, and all areas of our life.

Often, this has a dramatic effect on our relationships with others. Living from love makes it easier to accept others and have compassion for them as human beings, just the same as us, waging their own internal battles. We're less likely to judge, condemn, and criticise when we come from a place of love. Even if you aren't vocal in your attitude to others, they are likely to sense the change because people tend to notice when you come from a place of love, even if outwardly most of what you say and do is the same. Their *own* soul recognises the opening up of your soul, and even though it's likely to be unconscious, they sense the different energy that emanates from you.

The more you cultivate coming out of your head and into your heart, and living from Being, you will be growing the energy of love within you, you'll be making room for it to expand and deepen. When you start to feel more as though you are living in Being, and from love, you can actively put your attention there and choose to tap into the empathy and compassion within yourself, to extend it to others. This then allows you to create deeper connections in your relationships.

This is not about becoming a 'better' person, but becoming who you are meant to be, by living *in* and *from* love, which is the energy of Being. The key is to keep your heart open and notice when you feel you are closing your heart. You can sense that shift in yourself when you have armoured up your heart. All the ways of cultivating Being help you to keep your heart open, and live in love.

Dropping Down, Waking Up, and Letting Go

In the next section, we'll focus on how to *cultivate* the five states of Being, including love, because it's about developing something in yourself, with patient, directed effort over time, and nurturing the fertile soil of Being. These states already lie within you, even if dormant, and want to grow and be present in the world. They need your attention to help you in transforming yourself and your life.

There are many different ways that you can cultivate these states, and it's got to be what suits you, works for you, and fits into your life. The bottom line though, is that you've got to start somewhere, so make time to develop these states, because you can't move fully into your heart, your being, without them.

You start by entering the territory of Love (Chapter 4), which together with Awareness (Chapter 5) and Acceptance (Chapter 6), Gratitude (Chapter 7), and Creativity (Chapter 8) builds the foundation of Being. Through cultivating these states, you come to find Being within you. They are powerful enough to break the hold that your mind has over you and can help you stay out of your head, so that you become grounded in your whole body and the present moment, instead of lost in your mind.

KEY POINTS: HEART STUFF

- Your heart is your emotional centre, your core, and Being resides there.

- Every moment of every day, you choose what you experience, by whether you live from your heart or your head.

- Choosing your heart over your head is central to living in Being.

- Living in your heart leads you to your authentic self.

- You can cultivate staying connected to your heart when you go into your head.

- Living in your heart, you become your whole, integrated self.

PART II

The Five States
of Being

Chapter Four

Love

Love is about developing connections. It is communication. It is a dynamic place within you. It's not a feeling, it is the essence of Being. Love is the energy of Being.

Most of us probably associate love with feelings of love. However, these are really just the icing on the cake, an added bonus. Love is complicated and multifaceted, and therefore difficult to pin down to one definition. Fundamentally, I believe it's the essence of who we are, the core of the spiritual being we are; it's our true nature.

As love is the energy of Being, when we live more in Being, we live more in love, and from here, when we turn outward towards the world, we bring love into all that we do and say: into our relationships, the work we do, and into creating our intentions for how we live. Rather than just *feeling* love, we *become* love, we embody it. We become what we always were, but were only accessing sporadically, and on a superficial level. We still have feelings of love, and can discern between the different types of expression of love, but fundamentally we *are* love. It becomes the source of our personal growth and the vehicle by which we channel Being and our lifeforce into the world.

Our feelings of love, however, can help us to access the experience of the deeper state of love, as the energy of Being. Our feelings of love, when they're not obsessional and fixated on ideas about love, but when we actually let ourselves just feel them, take us into our heart. We *feel* the energy of love when we are out of our head. We come into our bodies and feel the swell in our chest, the sensation of expansion, of being filled up from within, as the energy of love infuses our Being. We come out of our head and into our heart.

Connection

Without connection to others, our souls wither and die, or at least they feel like it. It only takes the experience of real human connection to breathe life into them again. Our souls yearn for human connection, which is why many of us often experience too much superficial social interaction as soul-destroying. How many times have you been to an event of some kind, and found yourself engaging in banal chit-chat, and felt like you were going mad in your head with it, felt lonely amongst others, and wanted to escape? I have, often. Obviously, it might be a bit off-putting to strangers if you immediately waded in by trying to foster a deep connection when you've only just met. Small talk can be a way of breaking the ice before heading into deeper waters, but often it isn't. Unless we actively take the risk of pushing towards developing a greater connection, superficial interactions are what we experience instead. Worse though, is that many of us operate at this same level of surface communication with people we've known for years, including close friends and even family.

You have to realise that you *want* a real, honest connection with others, and be willing to sensitively develop it. You have to allow yourself to be brave enough to accept that others might not want that, but that doesn't mean you close down to it too. Whether or not they are open to developing greater connection is about how much the other person is open to it, not about you, or how they feel about you. Often, it's just them trying to stay within their own comfort zone. Maybe they've had negative experiences of opening up emotionally or spiritually to others in the past. Perhaps their heart is more closed than yours as a defence.

Connection is about being real, being yourself, coming from Being, and wanting to meet the other person in that space. It is actively extending your true self to another, even if it's only a brief or passing encounter you have with them. Then you are two human beings being open to discovering who the other really is, finding out more about each other, and engaging in real human connection, which grows both your souls. I would go as far as to say that human connection is our foremost need after being fed, clothed, and having a roof over our heads.

When the other person is also willing to open up and meet you in this place, then the possibility of connection deepening into intimacy becomes possible.

Intimacy

When human connection is a two-way street, and both people are willing to be real, be open, and be honest about who they are, and be ready to really be known and seen by another, then the beautiful experience of intimacy flourishes. Intimacy is an authentic, deep, human connection. You are allowing yourself to be truly seen, to be vulnerable and exposed, but with the promise that the person you are developing intimacy with will completely accept who you are, and will also be willing to open themselves up to be seen.

It's often thought of as something that is only reserved for sexual relationships. Physical intimacy is only one type of intimacy though and can be experienced alongside other types in a relationship or independent of them. However, having more than one kind of intimacy with a person is likely to deepen and enrich the experience of all types of intimacy in that relationship.

The types of intimacy most relevant to us, in exploring how we cultivate living from Being, are emotional and spiritual intimacy. Most people can recognise previous experiences of emotional intimacy. It's when we can talk to someone about anything and feel understood by them. You trust them enough to be able to share your emotional life. You can be open about your thoughts and feelings, and you feel safe in doing so. We're likely to have varying levels of emotional intimacy with different people, depending on an array of factors: the context we know them in, how often we have one-to-one time with them, how long we've known them, how much they seem open to emotional intimacy, how much it matters to both of you, and how much you are willing to extend yourself to developing it.

Next time you're at an event where there's usually just superficial chit-chat, take the opportunity to test out moving the conversation in a more meaningful direction. Ask someone something out of the ordinary or more profound. You might be pleasantly surprised by what happens.

Although it can feel scary to make the first move in developing greater intimacy with others, we tend to instinctively know who is most open to it – who might be looking for a deeper connection. We can test the waters by just opening up about ourselves in increments, then seeing how they react and respond. We don't have to dive in at the deep end. The rewards are great: to feel understood, to have someone hear us, and get to know us better, and not the version of us that we usually present to the world – the *real* us. All of this makes it so worthwhile to take the risk of being vulnerable enough to show who we are on the inside, to let another into our interior world, by trying to foster greater intimacy in our relationships.

Spiritual Intimacy

Many years ago, in my twenties, I felt a different level of connection and intimacy with someone, for the first time in my life. I wrote in my diary that night, 'Found it!' I didn't even know what *it* was and hadn't been aware that I was looking for it. I did have a sense that I had been waiting for something, though. That there was something more in the realms of human connection out there than I had experienced to date.

For the first time, I experienced the feeling of truly meeting another human being. Being seen and heard for who I really was – both coming from Being and connecting deeply in that place. Over five hours of walking and talking, I felt that I'd found the answer to something, to everything. *This is what life is about.* I recognised it as something I needed as much as food, water, and shelter. This was the route to being a whole, healthy human being. I had recognised my own soul and glimpsed the soul of another. It was the catalyst for my journey into Being. I had found a spiritual connection and experienced spiritual intimacy.

Closely tied to emotional intimacy, and usually evolving out of it, spiritual intimacy is where we bring who we are in Being into our relationship with another. We reveal our true self; we show our soul. The other is willing to connect with you there, in Being, from their soul. This might be with our life partner, or it might be with a friend, but when we do connect spiritually with another, we grow each of our souls in the process. We also get to know more of our own soul, as well as the other person's, and we become *soulmates.*

I don't believe that a soulmate has to be someone you are in a romantic relationship with. It can be, of course, and when that happens it's an added bonus, but a soulmate can be anyone with whom you have a deep connection, soul to soul, meeting in a mutual place of Being, and opening up your innermost self to each other. I have several friends who are just on the same wavelength as me when it comes to spiritual matters. Whom I can talk to about 'spiritual stuff'. I can reveal who I am in the depths of my soul, and they get it.

In developing spiritual intimacy with someone, you get to experience knowing and living from your own soul, and you strengthen your connection to your own soul in the process. As well as the joy and wonder that brings, it brings the feeling of truly knowing and being *seen* as the spiritual Being that you are.

Spiritual intimacy grows out of emotional intimacy, it's the next level. Having an emotional connection with someone, being able to be open, creates the conditions where it becomes easier to develop spiritual intimacy. It is what we are meant to experience in our lives.

> Spiritual intimacy deepens our experience of being the spiritual beings that we are. It is the ultimate goal of our existence as spiritual beings.

Love in Action

Love is a powerful force that infuses our whole Being. When you're *passionate* about something, you're feeling this force of love strongly. You are directing it towards a person, a project, or towards growth and change, and using the energy as fuel to create in the world from that passion. This is your authentic power.

The source of this force of love is Being. Living rooted in Being opens you up to letting love flow through you. You can have obsessional thoughts about something or someone and think it's passion, but for it to be an expression of the force of love it has to come from Being.

That's how you find what your *true* passions are – by living from Being and listening to the voice of your soul. Then you instinctively know where you need to direct your love, what you want to pour it into. You do it actively, consciously, even if it's at odds with what your thoughts are about what you need to do. The voice of self-doubt, questioning, hesitation, or procrastination is usually just mind-driven fear. Remember your mind wants to be in charge, it doesn't want you listening to the promptings of your soul. It doesn't want you following your passions, because that diminishes the power that it has over you.

You begin to bring Being into the world through love. It is the communication vehicle of Being, and it is our true essence. When we cultivate Being and begin to live from it, we connect with our soul, and this creates the space for love to grow and build, and to then flow out into our relationships and what we do. The more we do this, the more we live in and from Being and express it through love, we will have the lifeforce flowing through us. We don't need to think as much. We follow the dictates of our hearts rather than our heads, we become who we are meant to become, our true self – love.

Love isn't passive energy. Of course, experiencing peace and love together feels wonderful, and living from love brings the potential for lots of experiences of peacefulness, and gentle, loving feelings. However, living from love can also bring powerful experiences. Think about fierce love, for example, how you would feel if someone was being aggressive, cruel, or violent towards someone you love – what kind of fire would the love in you turn into? Or enduring love, where you go through thick and thin with someone, and maybe have times where you don't even like them but remain willing to keep your heart open to them. Or challenging love, when someone you love is difficult or hurts you, but you see past that and keep sight of all that is worthwhile in the relationship, and of your commitment to loving them.

Your commitment to loving someone comes from your soul's need to have a connection with others. When you decide to invest time and energy in extending yourself to someone, you demonstrate your love in your words and actions. By investing your time and energy in acts of love, you demonstrate your commitment to the other.

Acts of Love

Depending on the relationship, your levels of intimacy and connection, or lack of them, the way you demonstrate your love for others may vary widely. The way you are with someone, what you say to them, and the things you do with, or for, someone may feel like acts of love to you, but may not feel like that to them. We need to be sensitive to what approach is best by communicating with them and connecting as much as we are mutually open to. Check out what is required of you, *for this particular individual soul.* Sometimes someone can be challenging to love, because of how your relationship with them is, or their behaviours, but you do still want to extend love to them. Merely the willingness to just accept them for who they are, in all their flawed humanity, and accept wherever they are on their life path, is often enough of an act of love to let them know you care.

You develop your ability to actively love by coming into your heart and finding your desire to extend love to others. Then you come to others, as much as you can, from Being. Whether it's in developing your ability to be compassionate towards them, or empathise with them, or in acts of service to them, Being will guide you. Even just endeavouring to understand another person by *really* listening to them and suspending judgement enough to see their world through their eyes, is an act of service that comes from love.

I find it easiest to do this with my children. No matter how challenging it can be juggling motherhood, home life, career, social life, etc. – or how demanding and tiring caring for them can be – I keep in awareness the strength of my love for them and, crucially, how much I want them to know and feel that love I have for them. In our interactions, conversations, and just time we spend together, I keep this awareness at the back of my mind as much as possible. When I feel frustrated, angry, fed-up, or resentful of the demands of motherhood, or their behaviours, I try to remind myself to come back to that awareness. I remind myself to come back to Being, to love, and extend it to them, in whichever way suits the situation, or stage they are at.

Self-love

Unfortunately, self-love as a concept has often evoked negative connotations of people affirming in a mirror to themselves how wonderful they are – a kind of arrogant, egotistical self-regard. In the 1950s, psychologist Erich Fromm first wrote of self-love more positively. In his book *The Art of Loving*, he describes how, in order to love another person, we first need to love ourselves (in terms of self-care, respecting and taking responsibility for yourself, and coming to know yourself, e.g. being realistic and honest about your strengths and weaknesses).[6] This is the self-love which is now more recognised as being a worthwhile goal,

---

6   Erich Fromm, *The Art of Loving* (Harper & Brothers, 1956)

and a win–win for you as well as for those you interact with.

How often do you really practise self-love? We're much more used to judging and criticising ourselves. Think about what self-care you could begin to extend to yourself, and the difference it might make to your life if you did. It could be in showing kindness and compassion to yourself, or caring more for yourself physically, or carving out time for something that brings you joy. For me, a key one just now is letting myself take my foot off the accelerator and enjoying a slower pace of life, whenever I'm feeling pressured.

Self-love needs to be cultivated. Unless you've led a charmed existence to date, you're likely to have been bombarded with messages throughout your life that you've interpreted as, or were actually telling you, that something is *wrong* with you. That in some way, you're not enough. We've soaked up messages that we're not smart enough, attractive enough, productive enough, sociable enough, etc. All of these messages are stored in our subconscious and create our levels of self-esteem and self-worth. If you have low levels of these, you aren't going to be in a place to feel, deep down, that you deserve love, even from yourself.

Practising Self-love

No surprise that the key to developing self-love is coming into Being. In the next couple of chapters, you're about to see that through awareness, you notice what your thoughts and beliefs are about yourself and hear what you are telling yourself over and over. You begin noticing the rampant self-criticism that most of us have lived with since we were children. You come to see the pressure that you put yourself under, usually through just trying to be *enough*. Then, acceptance of yourself leads you to be kinder to yourself, not allowing your own mind to bully you. To know you are enough. I try to remind myself often of the anonymous quote:

'I AM enough, I HAVE enough, I DO enough.'

Having an awareness of how you think of, and feel about, yourself, then through acceptance of all that you become aware of, automatically takes you towards wanting to care for yourself better. You want to let go of unhelpful self-beliefs. You begin to want to direct your attention towards your physical, mental, emotional, and spiritual health and equilibrium. Over time, you can begin to create an ever-increasing circle of wellbeing for yourself, alongside coming to know who you are and creating the life that you are meant to live.

Journal:
Let's Talk About Love

Below are some of my journal extracts illustrating what I've been talking about in this chapter.

The Battle Between Head and Heart

After overindulging in food and alcohol at the BBQ yesterday, I woke up this morning feeling acutely aware of the reality of the contradictions between what I say I want, and how I live my life:

- *I want to lose weight and be leaner vs I ate and drank excessively all day.*

- *I value health and eating nutritiously vs I poured the poison that is alcohol into my body with abandon.*

- *I know that excess alcohol gives me crippling migraines vs I chose to consume it anyway.*

- *I instinctively feel the nasal sprays I use to treat migraines aren't good for me vs I still drank excess alcohol knowing I'll have to use one.*

- *I love walking and doing Iyengar yoga vs I don't do them the next day, or for a few days usually, if I've overindulged in food and/or alcohol.*

- *I feel the preciousness of time and want to be living every day consciously, creatively, and aligned with what I want my life to be about vs I lose time and myself when I drink alcohol or tranquillise myself with food because I press the pause button to deal with the aftermath of overindulgence.*

All of these contradictions cause me internal struggle and turmoil to varying degrees mentally and emotionally, and consume my time and attention, and distract me from focusing on growth and my spiritual self. Instead of my life flowing in a forward creative direction, this all makes it feel stop/start, and hampers progress and destroys momentum.

This is not what I want for my life. It feels worse because I can see what I'm doing and can see how destructive it is, yet I keep doing it. These are old, ingrained patterns. How can I do it differently?

Soul Nourishment as Self-love

I'm sitting in a café killing time before a meeting and listening to the chilled music, and I've just sunk into the moment. I feel very present, still, calm, centred, and me. I'm just Being. I realise that times like this aren't just about rest and relaxation, they are about feeding my soul.

Creating the right environment, or working at being present and conscious, connects me with my soul, my core, my true self, and that connection is nourishment. It grows it, and it helps me to grow spiritually and become stronger as a person.

Conversely, it has just occurred to me, if I'm in a social or business setting, and I'm not present and/or myself, I'm then feeding and nourishing my ego, and helping it to grow and become stronger. I'm in my head, interacting from my ego – I'm flexing the muscles of it and empowering it. I've also withdrawn from my soul at these times.

Disconnection

I feel estranged from most people in my life just now because nobody is talking about their soul, about spiritual growth. Instead, talk is of arrangements, the weather, material things, money, politics, complaints, irritations, or health issues. If anything emotional comes up, it's usually about fears. This feels like a soul-destroying way to live, literally. It makes me sad and depressed, and it feels like we're missing the whole point of life. Surely as human beings, we are meant to connect deeply with others. I crave that deep spiritual connection.

I want to be in a place of connecting to my own soul with other people around me doing the same, and even without discussing it or actively focusing on it. Just being in that same space together, as we engage with each other or do whatever we are doing. Even better, if we can talk about it and help each other in whatever ways we can to grow spiritually.

I'm craving connection. I feel lonely – not for company, not for socialising, but for deep connection. For someone to be able to share my spiritual journey and talk to about all this stuff. Not a romantic partner, just a friend.

Losing My Mind and Finding My Heart

After reading some of Eckhart Tolle's A New Earth[7] *about ego and mind structures, I felt very conscious and disengaged from my mind. I sat in silence doing nothing. I walked about the empty house very slowly and deliberately from room to room for no reason, just feeling the presence of it and how it*

---

7   Eckhart Tolle, *A New Earth* (Dutton, 2005)

feels. It all felt different and new to me as if I were visiting this house I'd lived in for fifteen years for the first time.

I laughed to myself. I thought that if anyone could see me, they would think I was losing my mind. Then I realised that is precisely what I was doing – losing my complete absorption in my mind. I had detached from it, and I was just Being. I was in my heart instead of my head. I was losing my mind and becoming sane. I was finding peace and finding my soul.

It's All About Love

I feel as if I can see the illusions of my own mind and the illusions of life more clearly, although I am not yet able to dis-identify with them for long. At the same time, I'm only able to be centred and at peace and feel like I am my true self for short periods. I feel like I'm in a kind of limbo, shifting back and forward between my head and my heart.

With this feeling, I get the sense that it's all about love. It's about living from love, giving love, letting love take the lead and be where my responses come from, instead of from my head. It's about being love. Holding within me the knowledge that nothing else matters, the rest is all mind creations. All I ever am is here, and now, one human soul in a human being, communicating to other souls encased in human beings. I feel full of love, and I feel really calm and at peace.

Being in My Heart

Where am I today? I feel a calm acceptance of life, of what is. I feel able to just be, and do, whatever feels right to do or not do today. I feel a sense of being in my body more than in my mind. I can see how complicated I make things when I'm in my head, how much I feel the need to 'sort things out'. It's as if my thoughts were a big ball of tangled wool that I have to endlessly try to tease out, to be able to relax after even just trying for a bit to untangle it.

When I am in my body, though, I feel like I am in my heart, and everything seems simple. My thoughts come and go in a more relaxed way, without me having to pay too much attention to them. Life seems simple lived from this place of peace and love. Being here seems more important than doing anything in particular. It feels that I can just do anything that needs doing in a relaxed way, without resentment, or irritation. It feels like it doesn't matter that a task has presented itself to me to be done, or what job I have chosen to do, or whether it's something I enjoy or not. The most important thing is still to be in this place of peace and love, in my heart, while I am doing whatever I am doing.

What else is in this place of peace and love? Acceptance, awareness, clear sight, truth, reality, solidity, strength, calm, contentment, knowing everything is OK, a sense of security, just knowing, and understanding. A knowing that we're all supposed to live from this place. Knowing this is who we are.

The only thing I need to do to get here is to notice my thinking and remember that this place exists in me always, underneath whatever is going on. Even when I'm completely

*lost in my mind, or I'm in emotional turmoil, it is still there.
It is waiting for me to come back to rest in it. To rest in my
heart, my soul, in Being.*

*Notice my thinking, notice when I'm in my head, remember
my soul, remember how it feels to live from here, and sigh
with relief as I come back to it. This is the journey from my
head to my heart to my soul.*

Love then, as we have looked at throughout this chapter,
encompasses the whole of our life. It is the core of who we
are because it is the energy of Being. It is the only way in
which we can bring Being into the world, into all that we
are and all that we do. The next two chapters detail how we
can build on love to cultivate awareness and acceptance.

PUTTING *LOVE* INTO PRACTICE

- Notice as often as you can during your day whether you are in your head or your heart. Over and over, make the choice of heart over head. Remind yourself that you *are* love, that it isn't just a feeling, that your heart is where it lives, and that you connect to love by coming into Being, through awareness and acceptance.

- When you're in your head but remember that you want to actively extend love to those around you, start by just really listening to them, or by simple acts of service, to let them know you care. There is a phrase that author David Brooks uses that I love, he talks about seeing others as 'fellow souls, rather than as other physical human bodies'.[8] If this was all we did in the realms of Being and love, it in itself would be transformative in all our lives. Try doing that and see how easily it connects you to your heart, to the compassion and empathy for others within you, to Being, and therefore to love.

- Be brave in cultivating connection and intimacy with fellow souls. Recognise any fear you have around it. Remember the possibility that the other may not be open to the level of connection or intimacy you seek and don't take it personally – it's about where they are on their journey, not about who *you* are. If you are in your heart, you

---

8   David Brooks, *The Second Mountain* (Allen Lane, 2019)

are coming from love, and wanting more open, honest connection. It is a good thing, a noble thing to try to foster. Test the waters and, if you need to, retreat and try again at another time, or with someone else. Being more open and honest yourself often paves the way for others to do the same.

- As you do all of this, make sure you also extend love to yourself. Accept yourself, warts and all. Forgive yourself for when you've been less of the person you really are than you had hoped. Be honest with yourself, be gentle with yourself, and be kind to yourself. Be your own best friend by supporting, encouraging, and nurturing yourself. Put practical steps in place to practise self-care. Above all, know that you are enough, exactly as you are. Tell yourself every day that you are enough, you have enough, and you do enough

KEY POINTS: LOVE

- Love is so much more than a feeling. It is the essence of who we are; it is the energy of Being.

- Choosing to live in your heart instead of your head is central to living more from Being.

- Every moment of every day, you choose what you experience, by whether you live from your heart or your head.

- Without human connection, our souls wither and die. Connection is about being real, being yourself, and relating to another from Being.

- Spiritual intimacy is true love and the ultimate goal of our existence as spiritual beings.

- Self-love needs to be cultivated for your wellbeing, and so that you can extend more love towards others.

Chapter Five

Awareness

Awareness leads you into experiencing what is happening in the here and now - around you and within you.

Awareness is about bringing into your consciousness what has previously been unconscious. Awareness isn't Being. It is your Being that experiences awareness. Awareness is a route into Being.

There are two types of awareness. One is awareness directed outwardly, which is about choosing to pull back to a place where your attention can have a more benign, observational, broad focus. It then takes in everything that is going on around you at any given time, all that you are experiencing, as opposed to the intense, narrow, focus of being locked in your head – with usually minimal, peripheral awareness of your present moment situation and circumstances.

The other is *self*-awareness of your own thoughts, feelings, and reactions *as they happen.* What you are experiencing within your own body and mind, physically, mentally, and emotionally. Over time, this leads to a greater and greater understanding of yourself.

Both types of awareness are also about coming into the present moment, whether your focus is outward or inward.

Becoming aware of all that is happening in the here and now, around you and within you. Both types of awareness can coincide or occur separately. Either can take you into Being, and there are different ways to cultivate each. I want to talk about outward-focused awareness first because developing this more general awareness of the present creates fertile ground from which self-awareness can grow.

Noticing

For me, the Master of the Universe on the subject of the present, on the NOW, is Eckhart Tolle. His book *The Power of Now*[9] is life-changing, as are *A New Earth*,[10] and *Stillness Speaks*.[11] When it comes to awareness, Eckhart talks about simply 'noticing'. That pretty ordinary word is so powerful yet gentle. It asks you to pay attention tenderly, unlike 'look' or 'stop' or 'attention' or 'wake up'. It doesn't bark at you, it doesn't scold you, it doesn't push or pull you. It offers you encouragement to drop whatever thoughts or feelings you are locked in combat with at any given time. It invites you to just notice them. To pause and come back to the present moment. To where you are in time and space. It invites you to just notice what is going on around about you – where you are, what is happening and how your body is feeling. It asks you to just notice, in a detached way, that whatever is going on around you or within you, you can still bring yourself back to the here and now, by becoming aware of it.

Noticing has helped me learn to come back over and over again to Being when I've been locked in thinking. It's

9   Eckhart Tolle, *The Power of Now* (Hodder & Stoughton, 2001)
10   Eckhart Tolle, *A New Earth* (Dutton, 2005)
11   Eckhart Tolle, *Stillness Speaks* (Hodder & Stoughton, 2011)

what I still remind myself to do now. By simply noticing that you're locked in thinking in the first place, it immediately breaks the spell and sets you free to pull back and notice more and more. When I've felt lost, confused, scared, or hopeless, the simple act of just pulling back to noticing what is going on within me and around about me, in the present moment, has been a relief. It is also usually the first small step in a positive direction towards Being.

When you are consumed by your mind, you can't solve the problem with your mind. You can only break free by coming out of your mind. As you now know, your mind wants to keep you there. It wants you to stay entirely absorbed by all its concerns, ruminations, obsessions, worries. Any small step into Being begins to give you a fresh perspective. To remember that the contents of your head are not who you are. It puts *you* back in the driving seat, rather than your mind.

So noticing is a significant first step and a great next step. Over and over, you can continue to come back to just noticing things. Noticing these things around you, and becoming more present, creates the space to notice what is going on within you. You start noticing your thoughts and feelings, and internal reactions to what is going on around you externally.

The beauty of cultivating awareness by simply noticing is that you can practise it anytime, anywhere. You can foster awareness in any situation throughout your day, regardless of circumstances. You are creating a spiritual practice for yourself, to use wherever you are, and whatever you are doing. It's that simple. In doing so, you are turning towards Being in yourself, and choosing to experience the here and now over experiencing being locked in your mind. With that one small, simple choice, made lots of times every day, you are putting one foot in front of the other, and step by step leading yourself into Being, and away from living in your head.

Self-awareness

Self-awareness – why cultivate it? One reason is to understand, to know, the reality of things, regarding yourself and your life. Not conceptual truths. Not an idea of what is true. A *knowing* based on unaltered reality, by seeing things clearly.

A lot of the time when we think we know ourselves it is in our heads. It's in ideas and concepts we have about our likes and dislikes, our behaviours, or our roles. It's in all the stories we've written in our minds over years and years. It's not in self-awareness, borne out of understanding and insight, with the input of the in-depth knowledge of our soul.

To really know yourself as a human being, you have to be willing to see all that you are in reality, not who you *think* you are. You may find out that you're not as nice a person as you always thought you were! Maybe you're more selfish, manipulative, deceitful, neurotic, resentful, mean-spirited, or demanding than you ever thought you were . . . AND THAT'S OK. You're a human being, with the capacity for *every* human trait within you. No matter how much you don't like that or don't see that. Every one of us has the capability within us to express *any* human trait. *Nobody* is as sweet, loving, kind, considerate, thoughtful, or compassionate as they might seem, or as we might see ourselves. You have to be willing to face the reality of your illusions about yourself – the fiction of your stories. Be ready to be uncomfortable if you want to be your *real* self, and you want to live from your soul. That is well worth coming out of your comfort zone for.

Every human trait, whether seen as 'good' or 'bad', desirable or undesirable, acceptable or unacceptable, is developed and cultivated, or neglected, ignored, and denied, through a complex web of myriad experiences, circumstances, events, relationships, decisions, choices, etc. Throughout our lives, they have developed and shaped who we are. As we looked at in Chapter 2, Head Stuff, it's who we have been moulded into by all our experiences. For the most part, we haven't been conscious of this conditioning by society, our families, and ourselves. We have been unaware of letting it become our story, our persona, and all that we believe we are. The beauty and power of cultivating awareness is that we also have the opportunity to see our conditioning for what it is. We can question what it's made us believe about ourselves, others, and life. No matter how far down the road we are, or how strong and entrenched our conditioning is. We can shine the light of awareness on it and come to see the reality of what it has created in ourselves and in our lives. We get to see that it's all just a collection of things that we've bought into, that we've taken on board, or experienced. It's not who we really are. In doing so, we understand ourselves better and learn to make better choices than we had in the past, when we were blindly following the dictates of our programming.

Usually, what you don't like about yourself, all that you don't want to be, isn't your 'fault'; they are your human traits and characteristics, and your conditioning. However, to the same degree, the qualities about yourself that you like aren't to your credit either. That's why we need to stop beating ourselves up about who we have become. We need to learn to focus instead on trying to understand who we really are, through self-awareness, but with an attitude of acceptance of all that we discover.

So, to be able to live more and more from Being, you have to be willing to apply yourself to cultivating awareness. Then, accepting the truth of what you see. The reality of things. Even though it might be uncomfortable, challenging, painful, make you 'wrong', destroy some of your ideas of yourself, others, or life.

Awareness is a vital aspect of the foundation on which living from Being is built. It is a crucial state to develop. In awareness you come to know yourself more and more: what you think and how you feel, moment to moment, what you believe, how you behave, what your motivations, avoidances, and/or sufferings are. You *can't lie to yourself any more* when you are in a state of awareness.

Most importantly, though, as you become more aware of your thoughts and feelings, you come to realise that since you are noticing them, they aren't all that you are. What is noticing the thoughts and feelings? Who is noticing them? The spiritual Being that you are. You come to know yourself as more than your thoughts and feelings. You come into Being. You inhabit it and know yourself to be much more than you previously *thought* you were. *This* is why it is so important to cultivate self-awareness.

So, where do we start with it? A good route into becoming aware of your thoughts and feelings is by first becoming aware of your surroundings. Just looking around you, observing. This brings you out of the narrow focus of your mind to a broader focus. Rather than being locked into *thinking* specific thoughts, you can begin to *notice* them instead. The same applies to how you are feeling – you can notice what feelings are bubbling up in you, or lingering in the background, as an observer. The other route is through becoming more aware of your body. Using your breath is a great way. You start noticing your breathing. Paying attention to it as you draw it in, and let it flow back out of your body. Not trying to control it, just really experiencing the sensations of it. Or you can run your hand over your forearm, or other hand. Just notice the physical sensations of it, as if it's a new experience to you – which it probably is. Feel being *in* your body.

> Using your breath or touch, you can then move to
> notice the thoughts or the feelings arising.
> As you can see, the routes to cultivating
> self-awareness are again about *noticing*.

Right here, right now, exactly where you are, and still doing whatever you are doing, i.e. reading this book! Be aware of where you are and what your surroundings are as you read, notice how your body feels . . . As I type this paragraph my hands are cold, and my neck feels a bit stiff, and I've got slight pins and needles going on in my thighs from sitting too long, and a niggle at my shoulder. I'm also aware I'm starting to feel a bit hungry. I'm aware that the sun has come out and that the computer is buzzing, and that I need to stop writing in about 20 minutes as I have to pick up my daughter. I also notice the subtle reactions mentally and emotionally to what I'm writing that bubble up, critical thoughts – 'Mmmm, not sure about that sentence, doesn't really work' – accompanied by a feeling of anxiety and of irritation at myself, then of wanting to go and do something else – all in the space of a few seconds. All of that awareness was there *while* I was still typing away on the computer keyboard. I didn't need to stop what I was doing to be in awareness. I didn't need to put my full attention on being aware. I was still *doing* while I was cultivating awareness, and therefore cultivating Being – one foot in doing and one foot in Being.

It's easier initially if you are someone who doesn't feel that you have much self-awareness, to start trying to develop it when you are on your own. It could be when you have total silence and solitude, or when you are driving, or food shopping alone, cooking, anywhere, anytime that you don't have to pay attention to having a conversation, or interacting with others at the same time. Just notice what thoughts come into your head and what feelings bubble up in you as you do whatever you are doing. The purpose isn't to analyse, criticise, or judge what you notice, simply to notice. In noticing you are becoming aware of your own mental and emotional states, of what you are experiencing as it happens. As you do that you begin to learn more about yourself. Over time these realisations will filter into creating change in your life, some may be aha! moments that excite you, some may puzzle you, some may upset you, scare you, or depress you. Most of your thoughts that you become aware of, though, and the emotional states this thinking generates, are likely to be mundane and repetitive.

This can be quite shocking when we realise how low quality and/or unnecessary most of our thinking is. All of this stream of thoughts and emotions that courses through us unchecked does not serve us well. It rarely creates anything meaningful in our lives and more often than not generates emotional states that sap us of our strength, energy, and vitality for life. The worst thing it does, though, is to consume our attention, and therefore our time and our energy. It keeps us locked in our minds, leaving little or no space for the lifeforce to flow through us, for the inspiration and creativity it brings, for love to expand, and for Being. Only when we've disengaged from head stuff, even just temporarily, can we create the space necessary for Being to grow and deepen within us.

Hyper-awareness

A word of warning. When I first started to practise becoming more aware, as I brought myself into the present moment and noticed what was around me and going on within me, I would soon get tense. I felt so hyper-aware of my thoughts and feelings. I would also be dragged back into my head quite quickly because I would then start thinking about what I was noticing. I'd be getting annoyed at myself for feeling a certain way or feel bad about myself because I didn't like what I saw, especially how I had been perpetuating the same old stories for myself.

Sometimes I felt that I had switched on this awareness and couldn't handle it. That I didn't know what to do with all that I was becoming aware of. It felt too much. I think that was because of two things. Partly what I talked about above, that the awareness would lead me back into my head, analysing and judging what I'd become aware of, creating mental and physical tension. Secondly, I hadn't got to the stage of accepting all that I was becoming aware of yet – which we'll come to in the next chapter.

So, watch out for this in yourself. Notice what you're experiencing. If, when you're practising awareness, you feel calm and relaxed and can sense your whole body, then you are in Being, and in awareness. If you are tense and feel locked in your head with your awareness, then you are not in Being. You need to notice your breathing and come back to a more relaxed state of awareness. Maybe initially focusing on what's around you, to break the intense awareness of your thoughts.

Stillness

For me, stillness is the key thing that brings me into Being. I seek it. I treasure it. I bring myself back to finding stillness time and time again. To ground myself, centre myself, and to bring me back to a sense that all is well in the world, and in me.

When I started my journey of coming more and more into Being, I only found stillness when I could be in silence and solitude and when my mind was quiet. In those days, that was a rare occurrence! Therefore, stillness was an infrequent experience for me. Whenever I did experience that sense of stillness around me, though, I felt blessed. It felt magical. I would try to hold onto the feeling of it, or the memory of it, in my mind, after the experience had passed.

In time though, as I developed more awareness, I realised that when I was alone and in silence, experiencing the stillness around me, there was also a stillness within me that mirrored that outer stillness. I then began to realise that I could come back to that stillness within me whenever I wanted. That it was always there waiting for me. All I had to do was notice my breathing, come out of my head, and let my attention gently rest on the stillness within me. It was a while before I realised that this stillness within me is Being.

If you haven't experienced the stillness within yourself, you can cultivate it in the same way I did, by first spending some time in silence and solitude. When you are there, gently turn your attention to your breathing, just noticing it. Then, when your mind is calm, and you feel you are in the present moment, become aware of the stillness around you. At some point, start to sense the same stillness within you. It echoes that stillness around you. Just sit with it, experience it, enjoy the feeling. Recognise what that stillness feels like in you, so that you can come back to it whenever you want. You might have to try this a few times before you can really feel it, but that doesn't matter. It's something you can work on and develop.

Stillness with Others

With practice, noticing the stillness within you becomes relatively easy when you are alone and in silence. However, in most people's lives, there isn't a lot of time, or opportunity, to be in solitude and silence. That's why it's essential to cultivate the ability to recognise the constancy of the stillness within you, *whatever* the external circumstances. The more you do this, the more you can draw on your inner stillness, for comfort, and calmness, and centring – whatever the external circumstances.

I realised this one day when I was writing on my laptop and feeling calm, centred, and in the flow of life. I began to become aware of my daughter and her granny bickering in the background, over some minutiae. As it started to bother me, I realised I had a choice. I could let it draw my attention away, as it usually would, and let myself get distracted and then annoyed by it. Then, I'd probably either move somewhere else, or ask them to calm things down, but I would still be left feeling agitated, and have lost my focus. This time though, I realised that instead, I could keep an awareness of what was going on around me as I continued to write, and accept the nature of it, but as a background awareness. I could put my attention on what I was doing, and also on the stillness within me. I did that, and the minute I found the stillness within me, I felt my shoulders drop, and my irritation start to dissolve. I managed to just keep on doing what I was doing, feeling calm amongst the chaos. I realised that I could do this more often in various situations.

Start noticing that whatever is going on around about you, while you are doing whatever you are doing, the stillness within you is always there. It's just waiting for you to breathe into it, and rest there awhile. To enjoy a bit of respite from the world, and your own mind.

> The more you seek out the stillness within you, the more easily you will find it, and be able to keep coming back to it for solace.

Routes to Being

As I've described, the Being that you are is what experiences awareness. Awareness is a route into Being. Mindfulness and meditation are routes to awareness. Therefore, learning and practising mindfulness or meditation helps you to cultivate living in Being.

Mindfulness

Mindfulness is really just awareness. It is something similar to noticing, but perhaps a more disciplined noticing. One where we come to see the world differently, the more we engage in the practice of it, and which connects us with the flow of life. It is slightly different from simple awareness because it is more directed and focused and can be used in a much more structured way. Mindfulness is non-judgemental observation, whether that is of your surroundings, others, or yourself. Not labelling, not pigeon-holing things, just observing, in a calm way. With mindfulness practice you train yourself, you train your mind, to see reality exactly as it is in the present moment.

You can learn and practise mindfulness in a more formal, structured way. There are many eight- or twelve-week programmes online, or books, to help you develop this kind of practice. It can also be started in small ways in your everyday life at any time. I think the easiest way to get into understanding and developing mindfulness is in noticing the movements or the physical sensations in your body as you do things, such as walking, making a cup of tea, brushing your teeth or getting dressed. You're just directing your attention towards the movements and the sensations, noticing them and keeping your focus on them. Just watching as each sensation dissolves and a new one appears. At the same time as focusing on the physical, just notice any thoughts that come into your mind or emotions that bubble up, without turning your full attention to them. Just let them come and go, without grasping to hold onto them, or engaging with them, or trying to push them away.

Keep your attention on the physical and let the other stuff just be in your peripheral awareness.

Even if you only manage to practise mindfulness for a few minutes here and there throughout your day, you are starting to create pause buttons in your life that are within your control – a way to reset mentally. The more you practise mindfulness, and deepen your experience of it, the easier it will be to slip into it at will. You then have a fantastic self-management tool for life.

There has been a considerable amount of research done in recent years on the benefits of mindfulness, for mental, emotional, physical, and spiritual, health and wellbeing. The results are incredible. It's clear that, for those who practise regularly, the rewards are comprehensive and far-reaching. It is well worth investing time and energy to develop it because, as I talked about in the section on time and energy in Chapter 3, you'll get so much more back.

Meditation

In my twenties, I learned Transcendental Meditation and practised it for a few weeks and then forgot all about it. In my thirties, I read a bit about Buddhism and mindfulness and learned mindfulness meditation. Again, I didn't practise it for long. Over the years, I've also tried guided meditation, walking meditation, and focused meditation – and probably some others that I can't remember. I always felt that I was rubbish at doing them. I'd hardly be able to stay out of my head, so I felt that it was a waste of time and didn't feel much benefit from it.

However, I now know that it doesn't matter so much if I go into my head while meditating. I just notice that I am and come back to my practice. I've been meditating most days for twenty minutes, for about two years now. Some days I'm still mostly in my head, and other days I feel the peace and calm descend as I sink into it. Most of all, the thing that makes me sit down to do it is that it reminds me of who I am. It reminds me that I am more than this flesh and blood. That who I really am is a spiritual being with the lifeforce flowing through me. In meditation I sense this more strongly.

If you haven't ever meditated, give it a try. It costs nothing, and there is much to gain. Have a look at the different types of meditation and choose what you think might suit you best. You might have to try a few different types to discover which is best for you. If you have tried it before, try it again. It can really help in cultivating awareness. Just be kind to yourself when you do.

See meditation as a tool to help you, rather than something you need to get right.

Entering the Realm of Being

So, whether you start to develop awareness and self-awareness through noticing, or choosing where to direct your attention through mindfulness, or finding the stillness inside you, you start to find the routes to Being within yourself. You start experiencing yourself as more than the contents of your mind, and you connect with the spiritual energy within you.

Of course, your mind will keep pulling you back into engaging with it. Of course, you'll have to remind yourself to come back to awareness over, and over, and over, and over, every day, only to slip back out of it again in no time. Unless you are an enlightened teenager reading this – and that would be great – you've had *decades* of reinforcement of your conditioning, over, and over, and over, and over, all day, every day. You've spent decades thinking that the contents of your head is who you are, is all that you are, and so has everyone around you.

Awareness is something that as we cultivate and develop it, it prods us to come back to it, and we start to realise more and more often when we have slipped out of awareness. It doesn't matter that we slip back into getting lost in thinking, it only matters that we keep bringing ourselves back to awareness as soon as we notice that we have slipped out of it, however long the interval.

Time locked in our heads is like pushing the pause button on Being. As soon as we come back to Being though, we instantly transform our lives, and ourselves. The second we are in awareness, in a moment, a realisation can come to us. We can see something different. We can understand something in a new way. We can know something more expansively, or more deeply – in an instant. It isn't about how long you spend in awareness, although it feels good to be residing there for longer periods, it's about coming back to it as soon as you realise that you're in your head. Time spent in awareness cannot be measured by the minutes of a clock or against the sense of time in our heads.

Journal:
Awareness Develops

Before we move onto acceptance which goes hand in hand with awareness, the following are some of my journal extracts that illustrate the journey of my developing awareness.

Awareness Begins

This morning as I did my half-hour walk, I managed to be really aware for more of it than I ever have, instead of just being lost in my thoughts. Initially, my mind kept trying to drag me into thinking, and I was engaging with it, then resisting it. Quite quickly, though, I realised I could just notice my thoughts come and go. I didn't need to engage with them. Then I could direct my attention outwards, to what was around me.

I was noticing the birds, seeing the beauty of the fields of barley, and absorbing it more fully. I also felt aware of actually walking, of my footsteps on the ground, and the sensations in the muscles of my legs. Weirdly, I felt aware of everything at once, not in a sequence. It felt like a new type of seeing – a new way of seeing the world.

In This Moment

I often want to be alone. I crave solitude. I realise it is mostly the silence that I want. I want the silence so I can be more aware of my thoughts and feelings as they arise, to keep myself centred, in the here and now. Often though, I end up in my mind – thinking, thinking, thinking. Ruminating on things, thinking about things that I've thought about countless times before. There's a feeling that I'll be 'OK' if I just have time alone in silence to sort my head out. Then getting mad at myself for not managing to stay in the present!

As I write, I have a moment where I realise that everything is already OK as it is. That there is nothing to be gained by searching, thinking, puzzling, in this moment. I've come to this moment without alcohol, or food, or sex, or walking on a beach staring at the sea, as a shortcut to feeling this. I'm just enjoying dissolving into it, into the moment. I can just be. I can just accept, and be in the moment, even though I'll keep slipping out of it. I can let go, but over and over, just keep coming back to Being, in the moment.

Out of My Head

I know I am in awareness when I'm feeling calm but alert to where I am, what is going on around me, and what is going on within me. I'm one step removed from my thinking, and so I feel more able to think about things in a less intense, more detached, relaxed way. I feel more in my body than my head.

Conversely, I don't even know I'm not living in awareness when I'm completely in my head, detached from Being, locked in my thinking. At these times, I have little or no sense of my body, I am just my mind. If I did pause at these times, I'd notice that my body is tense and my emotions are heightened, whatever I'm feeling.

Coming out of my head, and becoming more aware, creates a big impact on how I'm feeling emotionally and physically, for the better.

Mind Patterns

I'm becoming aware of all the many small and big ways that I create suffering for myself every day. I can see how my ingrained, unconscious mind patterns are creating this pain by generating impulses that I then blindly, automatically follow, in the behaviours that I then bring into the world. For example, complaining, irritation, anger, compulsions, impatience, etc. They then often set off a chain reaction of other patterns and behaviours, that can end up pulling me into a destructive or unhappy frame of mind for hours, or sometimes on and off for days, severely affecting myself and others.

It doesn't feel like suffering when I'm in those mind patterns. Usually, I'm so caught up in my head, in some kind of story or drama I've created around it, I don't realise that all the while I am creating suffering for myself. That I'm taking myself away from the peace and equilibrium within me, which I feel I most want.

Noticing the negative mental patterns as they arise, breaks the spell of them, and I can come back to Being and equilibrium until the next one arises. Each time I short-circuit them in this way, I'm reducing the amount of time I'm suffering, and simultaneously, increasing the amount of time I'm living in Being. Crucially, I'm disrupting the ingrained pattern of old mental habits, and making new ones.

Redirecting Thoughts

Yesterday, as I was driving for three hours, I was lost in thoughts of other times and other places. I could feel a mixture of strong emotions swelling inside me, and I felt like I could be drowned by them. That they were strong enough to pull me back into a place that I haven't been in for a while – a deeply melancholic, sad, lost, empty, forlorn place.

As I just stayed with it and noticed this, I realised that I was torturing myself. It seemed so clear to me that my own train of thoughts was causing me suffering. I was choosing to dwell and ruminate on memories that were igniting these strong emotions that had caused me a lot of pain in the past and were triggering the same in me now.

On realising this, I pulled back mentally and noticed my thinking. I realised that I could choose not to think about those things and direct my mind elsewhere. I did that. It felt difficult for a few minutes, but then the emotions subsided. I felt relief. I was left feeling mildly sad for a while. Still, as I continued to force myself to think about other things, it became very clear to me how much of my emotional and psychological pain is self-generated and how easily I can choose to stop doing it when I become aware of what I'm doing. . . now.

All I can ever do is make the most of now, and now, and now . . .

In each moment, I have the opportunity to be and make the most of where I am and what I'm doing. I can always prioritise Being. Being present, aware, conscious, creative, expressive, and appreciative.

I can only ever nurture, nourish, or be kind to myself and others, or be my best self, in the moment that I find myself in. Not in some near, or far-off, moment in my mind, where I plan to do what I need to do to be living the life I want to. I can only ever create that life NOW, over, and over, in every moment.

Awareness to Acceptance

Yesterday I felt I could just notice emotions arising in me. Annie was doing something that I was getting irritated by, and I noticed myself getting irritated. Usually, I would then be telling myself not to get irritated and get tense trying not to show her that I'm irritated. Outwardly, I'd try to be patient and kind but be feeling bad about myself for feeling irritated, on and on...

This could have a big impact on my mood, and/or how I was with her or felt about myself, for ten minutes, for an hour, or for an afternoon. All from my reaction to my own irritation.

However, this time, when I noticed myself getting irritated, instead of falling headfirst into the irritation, I just noticed it and stayed connected to Being. I noticed the irritation like it was a curiosity. I just let it be. I just let her be. Then I felt the love I have for her bubbling up, and the irritation began not to feel like such a big deal, and quite quickly it just kind of dissipated.

I managed to continue that for a few hours, so that whatever I was feeling would bubble up and I would notice it rather than engage with it. For a few hours, I was able to watch the comings and goings of my emotional states as an observer.

Without engaging with them, or more correctly, pulling myself back from engaging with them, as I did automatically as they arose. I was aware of it happening, so, I could pull back to observing.

I was able to stay relatively calm and centred whatever was going on around me, as various people and circumstances elicited particular emotional or psychological responses within me. It felt strange, but I also felt kind of amused by it, like it was some kind of game, and it made me happy.

Later in the day, I slipped back into more unconscious, automatic, reactive mental and emotional patterns. Still, I can so vividly remember how it felt to be the observer of them instead. I'm going to bring myself back to doing that as often as I can.

When we are locked into thinking, we are consumed by our mind, and our Being becomes nothing. Awareness has a whole other dimension and quality to it. It inhabits our whole Being and changes us. We become whole and fully alive when we are living in awareness because we have entered the realm of Being. *That* is why it's well worth developing.

Putting *Awareness* into Practice

- Stop. Several times a day, or even better, several times an hour, stop what you're doing physically, or whatever thoughts you are lost in, and just look around you as if you're waiting for something to happen, as if you must observe all that is going on around you. Listen to the sounds that you become aware of, listen to them with curiosity, as if you've never heard them before and don't recognise them. Do this as often as you can, for at least a couple of minutes. In doing this, you are beginning to practise pressing the pause button on living life as if you're on a runaway train, and you'll begin to exert control over where your attention goes.

- As above, as often as you can throughout the day, notice what thoughts are going through your mind, not analysing them, just observing. Also, notice your emotions, sense what is going on within you. You can do this *while you are doing whatever you are doing,* and you don't need to go anywhere with what you notice. Just notice and register it all. All the better if you can sometimes do this when you are alone, and take more time to stay with it.

- If you can carve out some silence and solitude for yourself, you can begin to cultivate finding the stillness within you. It doesn't need to be for long – even five minutes can give you enough time to still your mind and begin to recognise or sink into it. As I talked about previously, sit comfortably, then gently turn your attention to your breathing, and try to slow it down. When your mind is calm, and you're in the present moment, become aware of the stillness around you, and start to sense the stillness within you. Just sit with it, experience it, enjoy the feeling, and get to recognise what that stillness feels like in you, and see if you can sense that what you feel within you is echoed in the stillness around you.

- When you can find the stillness within you in silence and solitude, start to look for it when you are with others or engaged in an activity, or in a noisy environment. Remember how it felt when you sat with the stillness within you and try to sense that it's still there, whatever is going on around you. Breathe in slowly and deeply, and connect with that still place within. Come back to it as often as you can throughout your day.

- Experiment with doing things mindfully. Put your attention, in a relaxed way, on whatever you are engaged in, go with the flow of whatever it is, and keep directing your attention back to the steps, the details, the sensations, of doing what you're doing. Ideally, try to incorporate it into lots of the mundane things that you do every day, from brushing your teeth to driving, to cooking, to getting dressed. Anything and everything can become a spiritual practice when you bring mindfulness to it.

KEY POINTS: AWARENESS

- Awareness brings into consciousness that which has been unconscious to you.

- Awareness can be directed outwardly towards what's going on around you, or inwardly, to develop self-awareness.

- You begin to become whole and fully alive when you are living in awareness because you have entered the realm of Being.

- Along with acceptance, awareness is the foundation of Being.

- The core of developing Being is simply noticing.

- Finding the stillness within you deepens your experience of Being.

- Mindfulness is a practical as well as a spiritual tool that helps to develop awareness.

Chapter Six

Acceptance

Through acceptance, you say yes to the experiences of your inner and outer reality, which are offered up as you develop awareness.

When you consent to receive or undertake something offered, you cultivate acceptance; you say yes to living in Being. Notice that this definition of acceptance is an action; a dynamic, proactive choice, rather than a passive, benign way of being, where you do nothing, as it is often thought to be. The verbs 'receive' and 'undertake' also highlight the fact that with acceptance, you are actively committing to a course of action, you are *choosing* to accept your reality at any given time.

Acceptance, therefore, is a decision to acknowledge reality as it is. Even as you may be working to change things, you recognise that where you are in physical reality and in life, is just where you are now. Whatever is happening within you – psychologically and emotionally – and whatever is happening around you, are also all your current reality. Many people have trouble with this. Believing that acceptance somehow implies giving up, being resigned to the way things are, or pretending to be happy about a situation when you aren't. Acceptance is none of those. It is choosing to see without the blinkers of the stories we tell ourselves. It's about facing reality. Not kidding yourself or telling yourself whatever will make you feel comfortable, or right. Acceptance is about being brave enough to face up to who you are, where you are, and what your life is now. Accepting in which ways you may have created that, without shame or blame or reverting to familiar escape routes. It's about being open to seeing the reality of yourself and your life. The best way to understand what acceptance is, how to cultivate it, and live from it, is by recognising the non-acceptance that we all practise.

> Acceptance is experiencing what is *as it is*.
> Realising that it just *is* what you are experiencing,
> whether you like it or not.

Non-acceptance

The list of how we practise non-acceptance is endless. For most of us, it is how we live our lives the majority of the time. We get irritated by things not going the way we want or expect them to. We feel frustrated, or angry, at ourselves for not following through on our plans. We hate that time is passing too quickly, or too slowly. We get annoyed at other people for the way they behave, because we would rather they acted differently, in the ways we wish they would, or think they should. We might jump from being dissatisfied about one aspect of our everyday experience to another, then another, all day long. We continuously focus our attention on what we think is 'wrong' with whatever our internal and external experiences are at the time.

Likewise, when your mind is focused on future events, in anticipation of how you will be, and/or feel, or if you long for days that have passed, and dwell on memories, you are resisting accepting the present moment. You are resisting what is, and you are resisting living in Being.

Non-acceptance is resistance to what is. It is resistance to whatever you are experiencing physically, mentally, emotionally, spiritually, within yourself, or in your surroundings and situation, or in your interactions with others. All that you are experiencing just *is* your experience, and that can't be denied. Whether you like it or not, and whether you want to change – some, most, or all, of whatever you are experiencing. The route to finding peace and ease in each moment is to let go of your resistance to what is and accept it as reality – even while you work towards changing what you don't like, either immediately or over time. Resistance doesn't change anything, it just compounds the negative aspects of whatever you are experiencing, and gives you even more to deal with, or be unhappy about.

Part of the problem is that we live in a culture of non-acceptance. It's seen as the norm to complain, find fault, to vent our frustrations verbally, or sometimes physically. We see all around us conflict, dissatisfaction, anger, frustration, and violence – the external expressions of inner resistance to what is. Does this make us happy? Does it bring us peace? Does it make us feel fulfilled?

No, apart from the temporary release of venting, or comfort in the camaraderie of 'having a moan', it does the opposite. It fuels the fires of more and more dissatisfaction and becomes a harmful habit that we engage in automatically, and continuously.

Breaking the Spell

You cultivate acceptance by first becoming aware of how you resist *what is*. Start noticing the ways in which you practise non-acceptance as you go about your day. Just observe your dissatisfactions and irritations, or if your attention is usually on what's 'wrong'. Do this over and over, throughout the day, and you'll start breaking the spell of being *in* resistance. You are then *observing* your resistance, so you are one step removed from it. This is the first crucial step towards acceptance, the next is to notice how this resistance makes you feel, what it creates for you – physically, mentally, emotionally – and in the behaviours it triggers.

So, for instance, if your resistance is silently complaining about how much you have to do. By practising awareness, you'll start to notice the stories that run through your mind: 'It's not fair', 'I shouldn't have to do all this', 'I'm a mug', 'I'm getting taken advantage of', 'nobody even appreciates what I do', and on and on. You are now observing your resistance. How do these stories, this constant loop of dissatisfaction, resentment, or victimhood make you feel? Most likely either tense, down, depressed, angry, tired, lethargic, or sad. These states usually then lead us into behaviours such as venting, or acting out, taking it out on others by acting negatively towards them, or escaping into food/alcohol/ TV/social media, etc. Into whatever will redirect, soothe, or distract us from these uncomfortable feelings. Often though, we just end up feeling even worse, or maybe guilty, or annoyed at ourselves. All of this happens within us due to resisting *what is* in the first place.

So how does it play out if, when you become aware of the silent complaining about *what is*, you go down the route of acceptance instead?

As you notice the soundtrack of your resistance to whatever the present moment contains (in this case, the complaining voice in your head about how much you do), you begin on the road to acceptance. You can then open up your awareness further by asking yourself *why* you are doing what you are doing.

- Is it out of love for your family?

- Is it because you made choices to follow a particular path, or set your life up in a certain way?

- Is it that you haven't spoken up enough for yourself, because of what others will think?

- Or is it something else?

Just sit with these questions for a while and let them open up your awareness. Don't start a mental debate, or fuel the fires of more resentment, simply explore the bigger picture of the reality of what you are experiencing. Recognise that there are reasons for why you are doing what you are doing and accept them as being your present reality. Whether you like them or not.

Notice all that comes up, notice your resistance, and then *allow* it all to just be. To just be what it is. You're not saying anything is right, or anything is wrong. You do not have to take responsibility for the way things are and what you're experiencing. You're just allowing, and sitting with it, in Being. Even as you do this, and you might know that you need to change things, you can decide to do things differently. For now, though, you are just allowing *what is* to be. In so doing, you not only accept your reality, yourself, and your life, you are in Being, and that is huge. The more you cultivate awareness, and accept what you become aware of, and allow *what is* to just Be, the more you will be living in Being. The more you do that, so the more you will start to experience change, and grow, and notice the differences it creates in your life.

In the moment that you are in, you are just allowing reality, you are allowing yourself to fully accept yourself and your life.

Surrender

It took me a while of practising awareness and acceptance and trying to live in Being, and struggling with it, and still mostly living in my head before I eventually came to the concept of spiritual surrender. It doesn't have to take you as long as it took me! If you keep practising being aware and accepting, you'll be working towards it. Fundamentally, surrender is a deeper accepting and allowing, where you sink into the present moment and what is, letting it be. It's where you decide to be in a state of total non-resistance.

It's something that I felt I finally 'got' when I reflected on the word 'surrender' on and off, over a few days, and imagined the feeling of surrendering to the present moment. I felt my way into it. I envisaged how I would feel and how I would move through life. Then I tapped into this vision when I was struggling with acceptance and allowing. I would say to myself, 'What if I just surrendered to *what is*, instead of fighting it, and fighting accepting it?' Even wholly surrendering to *what is* for ten minutes was hard! Then, when I could, I would practise surrendering for more extended periods. It's something I still have to work at, but it's worth the effort for how free and peaceful it makes me feel. When you manage to stop struggling, drop your resistance, and surrender to the reality of the present, you feel a deep peace descend on you. You have a richer experience of Being, and you feel relief, because even if only temporarily, you've taken a break from the tension and turmoil that resistance to reality creates within you.

I would say this is the first level of surrender, and the next one comes when you are living more and more in and from Being, and can surrender not only to reality and the present but to Being. You allow the lifeforce to flow through you and guide you in all that you do.

When you become aware of how much time you spend resisting the reality of yourself and your life, you begin to see what you experience because of it, and what it creates for you. You also realise how much of your time and energy is wasted in perpetuating this non-acceptance. Acceptance, allowing, and surrender, are the steps towards letting go of what doesn't serve you any more: the illusions, the old stories, the destructive behaviours, the relationship dynamics, and the escapes you use in response to the pain created by all of those. You come to a place where you *want* to relinquish control, where you realise you don't have all the answers. You acknowledge that staying locked in your mind, always planning, organising, and getting anxious about things not working out the way you want isn't the answer either. The first steps on the path towards letting go on a grand scale begin with letting go in each moment, over and over again – accepting, allowing, surrender. You practise it in small ways, and eventually, it makes a difference in big ways.

In Extremis

One of my friends told me that she has a lot of trouble with the idea of accepting what's happening *whatever* the situation or circumstances. She went through a distressing, traumatic time over several years, and had to cope with experiences that would have most of us on our knees. She asked me how she could have just accepted things as they were, in the depths of her despair, and why she would have wanted to.

I want to address this here because I think most of us might struggle with this concept, even if our circumstances aren't as extreme. Whatever your situation or circumstances, whatever you are experiencing within yourself or in your life, acceptance of *what is*, is really a shift in perspective. It's an attitude towards where you are and what is happening. It connects you to reality. Acceptance is only an acknowledgement of the truth of that reality. In *fully* accepting your experiences as a fact, as your reality, the first thing you stop is your mental dialogue of internal combat against *what is*, and all the additional psychological and emotional pain this generates.

Rather than seeing acceptance as something in-compatible with the extremeness of the situation you find yourself in, try to see cultivating and practising acceptance as a supportive tool to help you manage what you're dealing with. Let acceptance be simply a peaceful place to rest amongst the stress and turmoil of the reality you are experiencing.

When you accept *what is*, you come out of your head and into Being where you are much more likely to be able to see things more clearly, and *instinctively* know the right thing to say or do in any situation, or the right course of action going forward. You have stopped the pain that living in non-acceptance *adds* to whatever you are dealing with. You are then much freer mentally and emotionally, and will have more energy to deal with the situation. You are then more likely to find your right path forward, at any given time – however extreme the circumstances.

It may take time and effort to move into acceptance, which is understandable if you've spent most of your life, like the majority of the population, perpetuating ingrained patterns of resistance to *what is*, by living in non-acceptance. When you do come into acceptance though, it changes the way you see things, and however difficult your circumstances or inner world, you can get some peace and space, and relief, as you take steps towards creating new experiences for yourself. This applies whether you feel you are at the mercy of extreme external circumstances that are beyond your control, or if your resistance is around other people, or your own thoughts, feelings, and behaviours.

Journal:
The Path of Least Resistance

The following are some journal extracts that illustrate my struggle with letting go of resistance to *what is*, and then beginning to build the habit of being more accepting of myself and what was happening in my life.

Non-acceptance

I spent most of today in my head, with my emotions in turmoil, and feeling tense and aggrieved with life, because things weren't going according to plan. Then tonight, as I continued to wrestle with frustration and resentment about not being able to do what I want to do, be where I want to be, etc. I realised that I set myself up for disappointment, frustration, anger, resentment, etc. a lot of the time. I'm so prescriptive about how things are going to be. I've decided in my head beforehand how something is going to be, and how much I'm going to enjoy it – even if it's something as simple as having the house to myself for a few hours. So, when things don't work out as I'd imagined, of course all the resentments etc. get triggered.

Then, I remembered that whatever the situation, wherever I am, whatever I'm doing, I always have the option to accept what is *and not create an emotional and psychological storm about the present, by wishing it was different. I need to remember in future that whatever is happening, if I accept it, and roll with it, I won't need to feel all those unpleasant feelings and create that mental and emotional storm within myself.*

Allowing I

I have been more honest with myself recently, accepting the reality of things, not allowing my mind to make them into something else, or noticing when it does. It feels like the tip of the iceberg. I think a process has begun of reality, revealing itself more fully than before, in glimpses.

I'm allowing it. I think it's happening because I'm allowing it. I'm allowing what is. Accepting it, whatever it is. Rather than letting a thought, or a realisation, or a glimpse of something, trigger a cascade of other thoughts and emotions. Running off somewhere with them, in my head, or pushing them away. I'm just noticing them and letting them be.

I want to try to allow more of this, but I don't really know what I'm doing, or not doing that has caused this shift. It just occurred to me that it could be my focus on finding inner stillness over the past few weeks or so. Could that be the difference?

Acceptance

Sometimes I'm just grumpy, or sad, or tense, or whatever. I don't need to analyse it, dwell on it, worry about it, or try to find a cause or a cure. All I need to do is just notice it, let it be, and let it run its course and, whatever the emotional state, watch it change and dissipate. Just the realisation of this has stopped me feeling grumpy!

I want to let my emotions come and go like the ebb and flow of the sea on the shore. I want my thoughts to drift through my mind like a river that meanders towards that sea.

Whatever my emotional state at any given time, it could come from myriad directions. I don't want to expend time and energy trying to figure out the source, I just want to notice them and accept them.

Allowing II

This morning when I was walking, I realised that in trying to keep on track with how I want to be living my life, I end up back in my head. Trying to remember concepts or things I've read or written, to remind me what helps me to stay in Being and out of my head! What is supposed to help me Be, takes me away from Being.

I realised that I would be better to just have one word as a reminder, to say, or just hold in my mind, when I need to bring myself back to Being. Keeping it simple. No thought required, an instant reminder, a shortcut to Being.

I decided to try this today with the word 'allowing'. Allowing.

Allowing whatever mental patterns bubble up to just be. Allowing any emotions, I have to just ebb and flow. Allowing myself to be who I really am, allowing that to be OK. Allowing Being. Allowing reality to be whatever it is.

All of this contained in the one word. All of it conjured up in one word. I only need the one word for today. Allowing.

A Place to Rest

Finding it easier to pull back from MIND (multiple inputs, non-discretionary! – I think I read that somewhere, very apt). Finding it easier to just BE. Noticing my mind spinning stories, catching the movements of my mind as it jumps from one train of thought to another, that it thinks will grab my attention better. Seeing the patterns of my thinking.

And when I pull back, the feelings attached to whatever I was thinking subside, in no small degree. I then feel peace, calm, and a sense of equilibrium emerging. I want to surrender to that. I want to allow it as often as possible. I want to live from that place and just BE. I want to rest there.

What Matters

Rather than trying to become who I truly am, I just need to remember that I already am who I truly am. I just need to allow all that I am and accept it. I need to notice when my mind is taking me away from the realisation of that.

Basically, nothing matters except Being, and love. Hold that in the present moment. Let it deepen and fill me up. Feel the joy of it, and when I can't feel the joy of it, feel the acceptance of it. The acceptance of what is.

Don't be drawn into the movements of my mind: the desires, the preoccupations, debates, dilemmas... into THE STORY of whatever is going on in my life. Whatever is happening in my life, I will deal with it better, and feel better as I do, if I deal with it from Being.

Who I am is a spiritual being, living in love, awareness, acceptance, and creativity.

Surrender

Surrender has just come to me as if it's a revelation. Surrendering the need to figure it all out, the need to have all my ducks in a row, the need to be in control, the need to constantly KNOW where I'm going, and how I'm going to get there. Surrender the need for anything except to Be. Obviously, I still need nourishment to survive, and a roof over my head, and people I care about around me, but apart from that . . . no resistance to what is. There is peace and solace in surrender.

Before now, I thought surrender was a mental relaxing, a kind of passive letting go of something, but it has hit me differently today. I have a different understanding of it. It feels more real, more tangible, and more like a decision: to give up the need, or desire, to wrestle with things; to try to figure things out. It feels like choosing to put down the mental weapons that I mostly use against myself. To retreat from the battle, with a big smile on my face. Choosing not to engage, choosing differently. Surrender feels like choosing a different path – the path of acceptance and allowing, in the present. No more struggle, no more battling. Surrendering to peace and calm.

The surrender I've been reflecting on for the past few days is also about giving up on the internal debates/dialogues, which are usually conflicting aspects of my conditioned self, fighting it out. Also, giving up my inner talk, where I attempt to manipulate reality in my mind, to make it seem to be more the way I want it to be.

However, underlying all that, there lies my true self – still, calm, at peace, content, and happy, just waiting for me to choose to surrender, and retreat from the battleground of my mind. To come back to the safe ground of Being.

Letting Go

Today I could really see, and understand, and believe in, what might happen if I really trusted in the lifeforce. If I just let it be and let it flow through me, taking me where it wants me to go, and surrender to it, without trying to 'figure it all out'.

I got a sense of not needing to know in my head, but of trusting a deeper understanding within me. I felt a peace come over me, freedom, liberation, relief, joy, wonder. They all came welling up in me from allowing that flow to just Be.

If I can just trust in this lifeforce and allow it to guide my actions, and take me where it will, I can express who I am at my deepest core automatically, by just trusting and going with the flow of the lifeforce. The only thing I ever need to do is focus on living in Being rather than what I'm doing, on staying connected to my soul rather than my mind.

The only thing I ever need to do is to BE.

Self-acceptance

- The best place to start is with *self*-acceptance, which is probably the most difficult but is also the most rewarding; it is this groundwork that makes wider acceptance more accessible. Through awareness, start to notice your internal critical voice, that in most of us narrates our life for us. This voice often tells us why we shouldn't have done this and should have done that, why we're an idiot, what we said wrong in a conversation, how badly others are thinking of us because of x, y, or z. It tells us that we're not achieving what we should, that we're lazy, selfish, stupid, on and on. Stop buying into it. Notice it, accept that you have developed this voice unconsciously, since you were born, and as a reaction to all of your life experiences, then refuse to give it airtime. Tune in to a different radio station, one that tells you that you're doing your best with who and where you are. That you are just a human being making mistakes and finding your way like everyone else. That 'perfect' doesn't exist. Give yourself a break and tell yourself that you deserve kindness and compassion as much as anyone else, then start extending that kindness and compassion to yourself. Stop beating yourself up for being you.

- Imagine you are your own best friend listening to all the harmful, critical content that spouts forth in your head. What would you be saying to your best friend? How would you be kind and comforting to them, maybe pointing out all that's good and great about them? Now do that for yourself. Learning to be kind to yourself takes time. Persevere with it.

- You'll have to actively derail your entrenched thought patterns and create new grooves of self-acceptance for your mind to follow. Still, just by wanting to change, and repetition, you will develop a kinder, gentler, more accepting attitude to yourself. This not only feels good and is a relief, but it also paves the way for more acceptance in different areas of your life.

Noticing Non-acceptance

- As you become more awake and aware, notice the non-acceptance that you practise, usually on repeat: in your thoughts, emotionally, physically, about your circumstances, of other people, of your life situation. Register this non-acceptance, recognise it for what it is – merely an attitude, a way of seeing things – and choose to let it go. Choose to come out of your head and into acceptance of *what is*, in the moment, without any meaning attached to it, or fear of who you'll be without this habit of resistance. Accept the reality of *what is*, and keep doing this, over and over, until it becomes a habit.

Acceptance

- Start with the things that you'll find easier to
  accept, and really experience what acceptance
  feels like, let it grow and fill you up, and sit with it.
  Recognise that when you are aware and accepting
  you are resting in Being, and enjoy just Being, even
  as you are still doing. The more moments of this
  that you can create for yourself, the easier it will
  be to cast the net wider, to what you find it harder
  to accept. In remaining aware and continuing to
  practise, you'll develop your acceptance muscles.

Surrender

- When you feel ready, reflect on surrender. How
  does the thought of it feel to you? What would
  your life look like if you surrendered to *what
  is*, over and over, and went with the flow of the
  lifeforce? Feel your way into the breadth and depth
  of surrender and let your imagination take you to
  what it would mean for you and your life, who you
  would be, what you'd be experiencing, what your
  world would be. Then try it. Let go.

KEY POINTS: ACCEPTANCE

- Acceptance is fully experiencing *what is*, as it is.

- It is a dynamic, proactive choice, rather than a passive resignation.

- You can accept your situation or circumstance, even as you still simultaneously work towards changing them.

- Noticing non-acceptance is the first step towards acceptance.

- With allowing, letting go, and surrender, we sink into the reality of life and go with the flow of the lifeforce.

Chapter Seven

Gratitude

Gratitude is far more than just being thankful and appreciative, although these are an excellent place to start.

Most people get that gratitude is about 'counting your blessings', and expressing thanks to others, or God/the Universe. Gratitude is also an attitude, a philosophy, by which to live. It's a decision, or a commitment, to see yourself, your world, and life, differently. It is also a way of Being. As with the other states, in cultivating gratitude, you come more into Being. You live more in and from it as you practise gratitude, and let it develop into an essential part of your *modus operandi*. Of all the states of Being, gratitude is most linked to accessing feelings of happiness and contentment. As it deepens within you, gratitude creates a filter through which to view your life and the world. You develop deeper and deeper feelings of satisfaction and acceptance. Gratitude helps you be more accepting of yourself, and others, and your life. So, if it's something that you haven't given much attention to, where do you start?

What Do You Want?

Most of the world, but particularly the Western world, lives in a culture of WANTING. Wanting, wanting, perpetually wanting, and seldom reaching the point of enough. Rarely is this wanting of the 'what's best for the greater good' variety, about desperately wanting the world to be a better place, or for us to be better people. The wanting is mostly about *things*, stuff, objects, or a different life based on material, financial, or geographical considerations. We want what we *think* we *need* to be happier. Unfortunately, this quest for happiness in external things puts our focus outwards to what we can draw in, rather than inwards to where the answers lie – to that which we can draw out from within us.

The very first step in cultivating gratitude comes from awareness. Awareness of how much you focus on what you want rather than what you have. Understanding what exactly it is that you want, and what you think it will bring, or the difference it'll make in your life. Most of us to varying degrees, spend a large part of our time absorbed in comparing ourselves, or our lives, to other people. The comparison is often unfavourable, resulting in envy, or resentment, that we don't have what they have, or we aren't what they seem to be. Often we focus on how far short we are falling from our 'ideal' version of ourselves. We envision ourselves as more attractive, thinner, being seen as more successful, or having more money . . . 'If only x, y, or z would happen, *then* I'll be happy.' We've all been there, done that, got the T-shirt.

Start noticing how your particular wanting manifests and how it affects your experience of life. What is it you think you need to be happy, and why is that specific thing the route to it? Write it out, as well as thinking it out – everything you want, big and small. Peel away the layers of your wants to find your motivations, behaviours, psychological and emotional pressures, and hang-ups. Whatever you discover, accept it. No matter how much you dislike, feel ashamed of, or embarrassed about whatever comes up. Be honest with yourself. Nobody else need know, and you are taking the first step in seeing the reality of your all too 'normal', societally conditioned, mind-generated wanting. You are also discovering what level of gratitude you currently live from.

As you become more aware of all your wants, and how much of your time and energy is spent dwelling on, or pursuing, those wants, you come to realise how little time you actually spend appreciating all that you already are and all that you already have. You come to realise how *un*grateful your heart is. Even if you feel that you do appreciate a lot that you have in your life, is it a background awareness throughout your day? Do you look at all your life experiences through a lens of gratitude? Do you go to gratitude first, before wanting, or complaining?

Complaining is the twin of wanting and grows out of non-acceptance of what is. Complaining is endemic in our society, and it comes from living in our heads. Along with wanting, complaining is the opposite of gratitude. Every time you complain you're saying things shouldn't be the way they are, shouldn't be like *this*. They should be different. They should be THE WAY I WANT THEM TO BE! Gratitude is the antidote to our culture of wanting and complaining. The late American author and motivational speaker Zig Ziglar said, 'Stop complaining – it bores everybody else, does you no good, and doesn't solve any problems.'

> Gratitude doesn't necessarily solve any problems,
> but it helps us have a better perspective on
> our issues and experience a happier life as
> we work towards solving them.

Head Wants, Heart Needs

In the wonderful book *Simple Abundance*,[12] Sarah Ban Breathnach says, 'If we are to live happy, creative, and fulfilled lives, it is crucial to distinguish between our wants and our needs.' Nearly always, our wants are generated by our mind. Remember how the mind creates and clings to 'the story of me' (see Chapter 2). Our wants are what we desire in order to add something to the story of me. They are what we consciously or unconsciously feel is missing from it. They are the things that would make us happier with our story. They would make it, and therefore us, more complete. More often than not, whatever we feel we need the world to accept, acknowledge, admire, respect, envy, appreciate, or value in us, is *because of* the story of who we are. We want to feel we are significant in some way, that we matter because of who we are, because of who we *think* we are, in our story.

On the other hand, if we are in our heart, and learning to live from Being, from our soul, we start to recognise our needs, rather than wants. We come to know what we

---

12 Sarah Ban Breathnach, *Simple Abundance* (Warner Books USA, 1995)

truly need, to experience feeling fulfilled, content, at peace, whole, sane, a sense of equilibrium, more present, more connected to our true self and to others, or even just a bit happier day to day. The best news is that meeting those needs doesn't require getting anything from anyone else, or the world. It comes from an inward focus, and only *you* need to do anything. Start becoming aware of the difference between your wants and needs. As you come more and more to live from Being, this becomes a lot easier. You start to discover what your real needs are, by listening to your own soul. We'll be looking at this more in the next chapter on creativity, as you get to the bottom of what you want to create in yourself and your world.

As you delve into discovering all your layers of wanting, don't get caught up in the rights or wrongs of the wanting, although it's useful to see it. It's not about *why* but *how often* you live in a state of wanting. As you begin to see your wants for what they really are, it's important not to judge or criticise yourself for having these wants or assess how valid they are. The aim is to recognise the state of wanting and to disengage from it. To shift to realising all that you already have and focusing on that. Then bringing yourself into a state of gratitude. Acceptance also becomes easier, the more you cultivate gratitude. They work in tandem, each enhancing the other.

Getting into Gratitude

Getting into gratitude starts with appreciation. Of all that you are, and all that you have. Not just in a fleeting, superficial way. Really create a shift in your perspective by reflecting on it over several days or weeks. Gratitude has to be more than an all-encompassing nod to being 'lucky' in life, that you occasionally become aware of, or express. You have to peel back the layers to *really* understand and feel what you have to be grateful for in the depths of your Being.

Imagine a set of several concentric circles, all within each other, from small to large. The smallest circle, in the middle, the bullseye, is where we start with appreciation and gratitude. This is where we realise that if we have a roof over our head, a bed to sleep in, enough to eat, and are not in any real danger of physical harm, we are already ahead of the largest proportion of the world's population. We have to be thankful for these basic needs being met, that we probably rarely give a thought to, that we take for granted. We need to appreciate that we are a lot luckier than other human beings, just like us, with all their wants and needs, but who have been less fortunate than us in having those wants and needs met. As well as these 'basics', expand this circle of gratitude to encompass the plethora of 'extras' that you have in all your belongings and comforts. Appreciate all the privilege you have in living the life that you live.

The second circle relates to health and wellbeing. OK, you might not be in great shape, physically, psychologically, or emotionally. You might be overweight, or unfit, or both, have a disease or illness, or psychological or emotional issues. Who can't tick the box for at least one of these?

Instead of focusing on them, or even as you deal with or seek support for them, notice what's *right* about your health and wellbeing. What wins have you had, changes you've made, or things you've dealt with that have created an improvement? If your health issues are not debilitating or life-threatening, then that's something to be thankful for. What can you still do, what can you still enjoy, *despite* any limitations? How much worse could it be? If the health issues you have are minor, then that's cause to celebrate. If they are more significant, do you have access to healthcare, and/or do you have support and information in dealing with it? When it comes to psychological and emotional problems, be thankful that you now realise that you can lessen the impact of those in your life by coming into Being, and you are going to do that – hallelujah!

Do you see where I'm going with this? It's a shift in perspective, from all that you don't have, and that you don't want, to truly seeing what you do have. It must have been a grateful person that said, 'Instead of worrying about if your glass is half full or half empty, be thankful that you have a glass.'[13]

The next level out, the third circle, is your relationships. No matter how far from perfect they are, what's good about them? Who are the people that make a positive difference to your life? What would your life be like without them? What experiences of love, or caring, do you get from your relationships? As you ponder these questions, no matter what thoughts and feelings of lack and resentment come up, stay focused on the good – even the smallest things. You're not trying to create a false picture here. You're getting real about how good usually sits alongside not-so-good, even in the most difficult of relationships. Pause for a moment to think about how you would feel if you had *none* of these people in your life.

You can expand the third circle out further by considering all the people you interact with day-to-day,

---

13 Anonymous

that you don't have any or much of a relationship with, but who serve you in some way: your grocery store checkout assistant, neighbours, taxi driver, etc. Spare a moment to appreciate them, even if you don't express it to them in any way (although that would be even better!).

The fourth circle is about how you create in the world, whether that's in your work, your home, or even in your self-development. Whatever feels to you like the thing you most channel yourself into or focus your time and attention on. (We'll talk more about this in the next chapter on creativity.) No doubt there will be pluses and minuses – whatever it is, focus on the pluses, for now. Later, in the chapter on transformation, you can begin to explore how you would like your life to be different, based on your true needs.

If you have a job you hate, do you have good relationships with some of your colleagues? Is your salary a godsend for keeping your head above water financially? If you're a full-time parent or carer, as well as it being demanding, tiring, or possibly not fulfilling you, why is it still worth it? What are the positive reasons for doing it? What are all the moments that you can be thankful for? If you're unemployed, what opportunities can you create for yourself in the spare time you have? What could you be doing that would enrich your life *in the meantime*? What can you be doing just for the enjoyment of it?

Finally, the fifth circle is about all that comes from Being. Hopefully, by now, you have a sense of the steps you can take to move towards living in and from Being. The more you put them into practice, and experience all that living from Being brings, the more you'll have to be grateful for. Appreciate the moments when you've felt aware and accepting or found a place of peace and calm within yourself. Maybe you've had a more profound experience of love when relating to someone, from coming out of your head and more into your heart. Appreciate any glimpses of Being that you've created for yourself by focusing on it.

Value what is always within you and cannot be taken away. Even the smallest of steps in the right direction are worth noticing and being grateful for. They are what takes you forward, towards more and more to be grateful for. The most important thing is always that you're going in the right direction, you are cultivating the state of gratitude.

Obviously, you can experience gratitude in any one of these circles separately, or simultaneously, and the more you work at developing gratitude in each layer, the more you expand your state of gratitude and yourself out and out. The ultimate goal is to experience gratitude *in the moment*, in awareness and acceptance, by living from a grateful heart. This is where all the states of Being start to come together, and how you transform your experience of your life.

A Grateful Heart

The more you work at developing gratitude and become aware of all that you have in yourself and your life, so you'll begin to feel a sense of wonder. You'll see things differently as you let go of ideas and attitudes of lack, of resentments, and feelings of being hard done by, as they succumb to the weight of the reality of all that you have.

When you develop a grateful heart, you seek out reasons to be thankful. You have a radar for it. If every cloud has a silver lining, you look for them, whatever is going on in your life. Having a grateful heart is a decision. Yes, you still need to work at developing it and expanding the circles of gratitude, but it starts with deciding that you want to live with a different view of the world. Deciding you want to shift from looking at your life through the lens of lack and longing, to one of gratefulness and appreciation. This brings contentment.

Sarah Ban Breathnach also said, 'I now realise that abundance and lack are parallel realities; every day I make the choice of which one to inhabit.'[14] Which one do you usually choose, and how does that work out for you? Do you want a different experience of life? Does living from a grateful heart sound good? It's available to absolutely anybody, including you. Choose to cultivate a grateful heart.

---

14 Sarah Ban Breathnach, *Simple Abundance* (Warner Books USA, 1995)

Journal:
The Growth of Gratitude

The following are some of my expressions of, and thoughts on, gratitude.

Everyday Wealth

At the most fundamental level, I know that I'm fortunate to have been born into my family, in our part of the world, and at that time. Due to those basic facts, I have love, privilege, comfort, and opportunities. My life experiences, good health, my personality and character, my mental, emotional, and spiritual make-up, all stem from this extreme good fortune. They are the foundation of my life and the person I am.

I appreciate the childhood I had, all the love I've had, and still have, in my life, and that every day I have a roof over my head, and enough food to eat.

I want to keep the awareness of all of this, in the background of my mind, whatever is happening in the foreground. I want to use this awareness to help keep whatever challenges I encounter day to day in perspective.

Growing My Soul

I get the feeling that gratitude grows my soul. When I bring my attention to all that I am grateful for, when I feel the internal glow of gratitude, I feel my soul expanding and filling me up. Maybe I feel more aware of the presence of it, of the spiritual being that I am.

Although it's only temporary, I believe that every time I expand my soul, it becomes a little easier to do it next time. It pushes out its boundaries and grows from the nourishment of inhabiting it fully.

This is Enough

This is enough. This moment is enough. I don't need anything else. This is always enough. I felt that so strongly today as I was out sledging with the kids. As we trudged through the snow and it was beautiful and peaceful, I came into the moment, and I knew it was enough. I stopped and just looked all around me, I took it all in, and it was as if time stood still, even though the kids were still mucking about in the snow.

The moment is always enough. I have enough, I am enough, and most things don't matter, especially thoughts and concepts and past and future, not when you are fully in the moment. I felt the purest feeling of peace and contentment that I had ever felt. I will call it to mind whenever I am craving something or unsettled.

The Gift of Peace and Happiness

Today I am thankful for knowing I can find peace and happiness within me. It's a gift. One that I appreciate. I didn't realise I had access to it for a long time, and now that I do, I'm in awe of it. That I actually get to choose to be at peace and be happy. That it's there within me waiting for me to direct my attention towards it, and away from the contents of my head. That I get to make use of it for the rest of my life. It's a huge blessing.

Appreciation of Today

I feel immensely grateful for all that today is. I am well. Those I love are well. I've got food in the fridge for dinner. The heating is on, and I'm warm. The sun is shining outside. I get to write. I get to be me. I get to find my voice and am not afraid to express all that I want to express. This is grace.

Grateful for the Journey

I feel so lucky, so grateful, to really, finally, be creating my life the way I want it to be. I feel the continuity of what I'm doing now. A sense of building on what I've done, and achieving something, rather than the stop/start, constructive/destructive, one step forward/three steps back that I've felt for years, due to the way I lived my life.

I feel a strong sense of mental and emotional equilibrium building, too – more balance, calmer. Even when I get anxious or down, it feels easier to bring myself back to this place. This feels like the place from which joy and gratitude grow. That just being here fosters them, and I can appreciate all that I have and all that I am, and allow my life to flow, in peace and joy. I feel so grateful for experiencing this in my life.

Putting *Gratitude* Into Practice

- Bring awareness to your wanting by asking:
  What's behind it? What do you *think* it will give
  you? Recognise that you are in your head with
  your wanting and come back to your heart. Start
  stripping back your wants to discover what you
  really need. Create a needs list that you can add to
  whenever you recognise more of what you truly
  need, as you begin to live more in Being and hear
  your soul. Your needs will help you achieve your
  vision of all that you and your life can be, alongside
  all that you already have.

- Start a gratitude journal. I resisted this for a
  long time. I'd think, *'I know I'm lucky,* so I don't
  need to spend time writing it down.' I was
  wrong. When I did start using one regularly, I
  noticed how much more 'attuned' I became to
  my blessings. It kept them at the forefront of my
  mind. Whether you want to use an actual journal,
  or just jot it down somewhere, start writing
  down everything that you are currently grateful
  for. Think about all that you take for granted and
  name it, acknowledge it. Go through the five
  circles, get it all down, then keep adding to your
  list. You don't need to start from the basics every
  time, and you don't need to write in it every day,
  but make it a regular practice, and notice the
  difference it makes to your life. Then, at times
  when you're feeling a sense of lack or longing,

take your list and remind yourself of all that you can be grateful for.

- Express gratitude in whatever way you want, to as many people as you can, and do it as often as possible. NOT just a polite 'thank you' but a sincere, heartfelt expression of appreciation.

- Every day pause for thought on those less fortunate than yourself, that haven't had your blessings, and realise there are a lot of them.

KEY POINTS: GRATITUDE

- Gratitude isn't merely a feeling of being lucky or fortunate.

- You need to consciously develop gratitude and nurture it.

- Gratitude is a lens through which you get a different view of your world.

- We live in a culture of wanting; gratitude brings us to an understanding of our true needs.

- There are circles of gratitude that you can expand out to eventually live from a grateful heart.

Chapter Eight

Creativity

When you are in a state of creativity, and pulling all the other strands of Being together, you enter the arena of vast possibility. You are fulfilling the promise of your unique potential in WHATEVER you do.

Historically, producing a work of art, whether it is a painting or sculpture, piece of music, a poem, or some other form of writing, has usually been seen as the sole definition of creativity. Someone who is an artist, or into making crafts, or a filmmaker, would be generally thought of as a creative person and, of course, they are. However, I would say that we all are. There is no such thing as a creative person, as opposed to a non-creative one. We ALL have creativity within us, and not just the ability to create artistically.

Any vehicle that you use to bring your Being into the world is your creativity being expressed.

We constantly create in the world around us, but we don't recognise it. We might spend time and energy on creating a lovely home, in our job or business, in sport, in our communities. You are drawing out that which is within you, from your soul, or from love, as a way to connect and communicate. Maybe it's from a need to do things differently or to create a different environment for yourself or others, or different experiences of life. You do it whenever you put *yourself* into something. When your input creates something different, you put your stamp on it. This is the final piece of the jigsaw of Being as creativity leads you to fully becoming your true self, and expressing from your soul in the world.

The best analogy I've ever heard to describe our soul goes something like this. Imagine humans are lamps. When we're born, we're plugged into our source of electricity – God/universal energy/spirit/lifeforce. The more we use this lifeforce energy, the more it will flow into us, and illuminate our lives. We throw out the light that this energy generates into the world around us, in all that we do. When we die, the lamp (us) is unplugged again from the power source. The light, the lifeforce that infused us, is gone, and our body is the shell that's left.

I believe that the soul is where the creative lifeforce meets us as an individual, and that we connect with it through our heart, in Being. When you live more from your heart, you begin to recognise, connect with, and experience your soul. As you draw on it, it flows through who you are in your heart, in your head, in your character and personality, and through the filter of your life experiences. These all affect how you then express that lifeforce in the world, how you create in the world.

Creativity is your unique expression of your own soul.

Creativity is not something we *do*. It's not about *making things*. That's only one form of creative expression. It's one of our natural states of Being that we don't often really recognise because our attention is caught by all that is in our heads.

We are all *creative beings*. We have ideas, we grow, we solve problems, we find new ways of doing things, we adapt, we change things in ourselves and in our lives. We get creative in overcoming challenges whenever we put our true selves into what we do and create as an expression of Being. We already express ourselves in the world every day. The difference is whether we express ourselves from our heads – in words and actions that are generated by our fears, anxieties, shoulds and should nots – or from Being, from our souls, in awareness, acceptance, love, and gratitude. That's the choice we make in every moment, countless times a day. It's where we choose to live from that creates who we become day by day, and which creates our world.

Creativity is our growth impulse, driving us to expand our experiences and improve them. Most of all, it implores us to bring who we are in our souls into alignment with who we are in the world. To let ourselves be seen for who we really are. Even if we're not in connection with our own souls, we can see this impulse at work all around us. Who we are in our head tries to express who it is by latching onto things. How often are we eager to tell someone, 'I *love* this', 'I don't like that . . . it's not *me*', 'I'm obsessed by the colour red', 'Cricket is my passion', . . . whatever is the *thing*. What we are really saying is, *this,* is what I'm about.

This represents me, *this* is why I'm different, unique, and/ or special.

This is all fine, and not detrimental, as long as we realise that it's coming from our head, not our soul. It may be that when you are living more from Being some of these things still apply as they align with who you are in your soul, but they might not. They might no longer feel significant or interest you any more, as you discover who you really are, and follow your true instincts about what is right for you.

The State of Creativity

How do you know when you are in a creative state? This applies whether we're talking about artistic creativity or creativity in general. Being in a state of creativity can bring with it many of the experiences that come from Being: positivity, inspiration, instinctive action, aliveness/vitality, intuition, openness to people and experiences, a sense of alignment, serendipity, joy, or feelings of satiety, expansion, momentum, or equilibrium.

It is so worth cultivating your own creativity because when you are in a creative state, you are drawing on the innate power that comes from Being. It might help you be braver, surer, or more confident in what you do, or feel stronger, more capable, think outside the box, have a sense of knowing what's right, but most of all, you will develop trust in your own instincts for how you want to live. All of that confers more of an experience of ease, and satisfaction, in our lives, because we're less in our heads. We're not feeling the need to strategise and figure it all out if we're responding instinctively.

Creativity is the easiest state to cultivate. Why? It is already active within you and emerges naturally as you learn to live in Being. In cultivating the other four states of Being, you come to know your own soul, and creativity flows from here. That being said, you still need to cultivate the ability to recognise it and develop trust in your creative instincts. To help you in expressing your creative self, and living creatively, the attitude you want to develop is one that you might have if you were a close, supportive, encouraging, but firm, friend to someone. You tell yourself that it's OK to follow your own instincts, that you can trust them when they come from a state of Being. That you are becoming your true self and that's got to be a good thing. If it feels scary, or you feel vulnerable, that's OK too, it doesn't mean you can't still do what you need to do.

Often the barriers that come up when we express more of our creative self are fear of feeling exposed, being judged, drawing attention to ourselves, negative feedback, etc. Recognise these barriers as fear generated by your mind. Be *aware* of them, and accept them for what they are – phantoms. Come back into your heart, knowing that you can let go of them, and still do what you were going to do. I often quote the title of a great book I read years ago, by Susan Jeffers, *Feel the Fear and Do It Anyway*,[15] to myself; it reminds me to stay focused on what I want to create, to be brave, and not allow my fears to derail me. That just because I feel scared or vulnerable doesn't mean I can't do what I plan, or most want to do.

The more often you do this, the more momentum you create, which takes you forwards, towards all that you want

---

15 Susan Jeffers, *Feel the Fear and Do It Anyway* (Arrow Books, 1991)

to achieve, and it silences your inner demons each time you do. You then come to live more and more creatively. This is how we grow. We expand all that we are *in Being* and open ourselves up to experiencing more of what we already are, becoming uniquely and authentically ourselves.

Cultivating Creativity

Allowing your creativity to flow is about opening up to life and allowing it to flood into, and through you, embracing all that it encompasses. You absorb all the possibilities that it contains and draw on the energy of this aspect of the lifeforce. It's being willing to push the boundaries and do whatever you need to do to feel that you are being fully yourself, or at least working towards it. It's about being honest with yourself in what drives you, and what you feel compelled to do, from your soul. Not letting yourself get in your own way or make excuses as to why you can't do what you suspect you must. It's allowing the light that is within you to shine as brightly as it wants to.

Be willing to be brave and be curious. Be interested in life, become a detective in search of what feeds your creative spirit and what starves or squashes it. Notice, notice, notice. Follow your nose and assemble the components of the vehicle that is going to take you where you want to go. You'll know what's right for you because it will feel right, in your gut, in your soul. You'll recognise the resonance of it with who you are, and what you want your life to be about.

Lastly, support others to do the same, whenever you can. At every opportunity, recognise and affirm when others are endeavouring to cultivate living creatively, when they are stretching into being more fully themselves.

Appreciate that and accept it – simply because you know how important it is for every individual to nurture their own creative spirit, whatever that looks like for them. Don't judge, don't criticise. Allow, as you would want them to do for you.

> Creativity breeds more creativity,
> and recognising others' creative endeavours,
> keeps you more aligned with your own.

Creating Your World

We looked at wants versus needs in the previous chapter on gratitude. The needs list that you began to form is an excellent place to start in figuring out what you want to create in the world. What feels most essential to you? What's important? Who do you *need* to be completely yourself and feel fulfilled? What makes you feel good, and as if you are your true self? What makes your soul sing? We'll go into this more in the next chapter, Transformation, where you'll create a clearer vision of what you want to create, but if you haven't done much of this before, here is where you start exploring what makes you tick.

Your hopes and dreams are yours. No matter how much they go off on a tangent from where you are now. No matter how much they might lead you down roads that others don't approve of or won't support. Don't think about the practicalities at this stage. You are mining for information just now. You're digging down into the depths of your Being to drag all that is there into the light. As you do this, more will bubble up to the surface, into your awareness, the more time you spend in a state of Being. They are all pieces of the jigsaw puzzle of you. The elements that you need to come together to create yourself and your world from your soul.

Artistic Creativity

Coming back to the more usual way of thinking of creativity, as artistic expression, is this any different in cultivating, are there other considerations? Yes, definitely, not that it makes it anymore 'special' a way to be creating in the world. It's not more significant or essential. Many incredibly creative people don't express themselves artistically. It's just that when someone does, it's usually more visible. Therein lies the primary consideration. With artistic expression, you are putting your creativity, and your true self, out there into the world, by whichever route, and in whichever format you choose, or that chooses you!

To be willing to put what you create at the mercy of others feedback, judgements, and potential criticism is to expose your true self. You're revealing what's on the inside of you, that which often hasn't ever seen the light of day before. Even if it's not apparent or explicit, and you might not even know what it is that you are directing outwards from within, you get the sense that you are baring your soul. Notice these feelings, notice the fear and anxiety, and do what you need to do anyway. The important thing is that it *feels* like you've expressed what you want or need to communicate, in the way that you want to express it. If you feel that it comes from Being, then you're putting your soul into what you do, and it will land where it's supposed to. It will reach other souls. Trust in that and be brave, letting go of the fears.

In writing this book, I'm *hugely* exposing myself. I've even chosen to include extracts from my journals. It doesn't get much more revealing than that! I'd be lying if I said I didn't give it a second thought initially, but however scary it felt to do, I knew it was essential, as they are so illustrative of the process of coming into Being. In doing so, I'm saying, 'Think what you will, like what I'm revealing or don't, but it's just unapologetically me. It's who I am, in all my flawed, neurotic humanity.' It's about being able to connect with others from a real place and create meaning and direction out of chaos and flux, with the hope that where it lands it will resonate in some way, and support, comfort, or affirm others.

My biggest joy in the creative process is just writing. Feeling the joy of knowing that I am expressing my true self creatively. Dropping down into myself and sensing the exact words that will most precisely convey my meaning. Feeling the thrill of that act of creativity. Even when it's difficult, even when I feel uninspired, or I'm frustrated that I'm not quite capturing what I am trying to, or when I'm distracted or procrastinating. Those times pale into the background, and feel insignificant, compared to the times when I experience being 'in the zone.' When I'm feeling the flow of my creative self. *Then* it feels like magic. It feels like I am doing what I was born to do. I feel a deep sense of gratitude that I get to experience this state. I know that this is what I *must* do to feel complete and truly myself.

Being in this creative state of *flow* is to experience what Mihaly Csikszentmihalyi describes as 'the joy of the process of total involvement in life'. In his brilliant book *Flow: The Psychology of Happiness*,[16] he drew over twenty years of research into new psychological theories of *optimal experience*, whereby in a state of flow we experience 'a sense of exhilaration, a deep sense of enjoyment that is long cherished and that becomes a landmark in memory.'

Obviously, this state of flow can happen in other areas of life, not just artistic endeavour, but I would argue that it's likely to happen most keenly when we are expressing our creative selves. Bringing our true self to what we do. Whether expressing artistically or in other creative pursuits. All this being said, it still takes effort and application, and it can still feel challenging, but the momentum of experiencing flow pulls you forward, and you *want* to apply yourself and put in the required effort.

As with general creativity, you have to be willing to look within: to be brave, curious, and resilient. You have to accept that feelings of vulnerability come with the territory and be honest with yourself. It all becomes so much easier when you cultivate living in Being. *From there,* trust your instincts, learn to recognise the voice of your soul, in all its guises: the promptings, urges, crazy what ifs, a sense of knowing, or full-blown, detailed visions.

There are lots of great books, workshops, videos, and exercises, which can you help to cultivate artistic creativity, and you'll find some listed at the end of this book.

---

16   Mihaly Csikszentmihalyi, *Flow: The Psychology of Happiness* (Harper Perennial Modern Classics, 2008)

Journal:
My Creative Path

These are some of the extracts from my journals that I feel most illustrate the process of cultivating creativity.

Cultivating My Creative Self

I want to write something about my frustration in seeing and knowing more of my soul, but not feeling able to align my outer self/personality with it. There feels like a disconnect. I remember a quote by Gary Zukav: 'When the personality comes fully to serve the energy of the soul, that is authentic power.'[17]

I start to feel it happening, and then I get pulled into life stuff. I think that I lose my true self in the day-to-day busyness of life.

It feels like two things are going on. One is my ability to connect with my soul and feel the spiritual being that I am. The second is to then express that in the world through my personality. I'm getting better at doing the first. I'm hoping that living as much as I can in Being helps with the latter. That Being will more naturally flow into my life through my personality, the more that I live my life from it. I don't need to try to have my personality serve the energy of my soul, it will do it automatically, the more I live in Being.

When it does, when the spiritual energy of my soul flows out of me through who I am into the world, shaped by my unique personality, experiences, life-situation, etc. THIS is

---

17 Gary Zukav, *The Seat of the Soul* (Ebury, 1991)

my uniqueness. This is how everyone expresses their own uniqueness.

It feels powerful for me to see it this way and makes much more sense. It solidifies for me why I need to make time for spiritual practice, to build up my amount of time living in Being.

Time spent meditating, reading, or writing spiritually, being in peace and stillness, is all about keeping the connection, keeping the channel open for your soul to flow into your life. We need to find more and more ways to incorporate that into our lives every day, as often as possible, and then the lifeforce helps us create a different world for ourselves.

We're All the Same, and We're All Unique

Who I truly am is exactly the same as everyone else. We are all the same in our essence, in our spirit, in our soul. The difference comes in how that manifests through us into the world, what it creates, what forms it takes.

In finding our true self, we are connecting with our soul, the lifeforce within us. How we then choose to express that in our way is our uniqueness and our gift to the world.

Our uniqueness and our special purpose on earth come not from us being different from others, it comes from the exact same source as the creativity of every other person that has ever lived. Each of us is just expressing it our way.

Our own life journeys, experiences, history, culture, conditioning, personalities, etc. will shape how we express the lifeforce in the world. How we communicate it may change throughout our lives. However, the energy, the inspiration, the force behind it all, coming through each of us, in ALL of our creative endeavours, is the same – the one lifeforce.

Creating New Habits

I've had enough of the destructiveness of my old habits and behaviours. The way that they've become my default. That no matter how far I've gone in the direction of creating positive change when I slip back into these old patterns, I feel back at square one. Even though, when I can get a better perspective again, I realise I'm not. It does feel like that at the time.

These old patterns get me into a place where I can't enjoy any progress I've made. I can't just enjoy and appreciate all that I have and all that I am – even with any issues or problems. They take me to an unhappy, anxious place of ruminating, obsessing, and wanting escape, instead of just living.

I want to break these old patterns. I want to have balance, equilibrium, peace, and continuity.

Things to remember that might help:

- I need to create new habits, and this will take time.

- I can create habits that help me create my dreams.

- Habits are building blocks, and every day I can continue to build bit by bit.

- *What I do NOW creates my future.*

- *I want to create WELLNESS and enjoy creating it.*

- *Recognise that my thought patterns are head stuff, and are from unconscious conditioning, and aren't who I am.*

Creating Change NOW

Change doesn't happen in the future. I can't create what I want in the future. I can only create it now. I can only create it choice by choice now. Every choice I make now, in each moment, is creating my future. It is not creating a concept of how my future is going to be. It is actually creating it in every moment, choice by choice.

The Experience of Flow

When I let my true self come into the world through me, I feel inspired and create with ease, and joy, and flow. It feels right, and it feels that I'm doing what I am meant to do. It feels like I'm Being. That I'm fulfilling my potential as a human being by being a vessel for the lifeforce to flow into me and out of me again. For it to be expressed in the world. To be a vehicle for the concrete expression of the lifeforce in the world. Rather than just a knowing, I experience something tangible. I feel and experience the energy of it.

First and Foremost - Being

I realise more clearly that to be able to achieve my vision, I need to foster all aspects of Being daily. I need to foster being in a place of awareness, acceptance, living from love, gratitude, and creativity, as much as possible. Then from this place of Being, I will do what I need to do, in the way that I need to do it, to create my vision in reality.

Aligned to that, yesterday it came to me that I want to endeavour to spend my time just being awake and aware, or reminding myself of my visions as I do. In doing this, I'll draw myself forwards, towards them, and pull them towards me. Depending on what feels most important at any given time, I can focus more on different aspects of my vision – my writing, other work, relationships, health etc. – letting my instinct guide me on where I most need to direct my attention.

In doing this, I'll be directing my time, and my mental, emotional, and spiritual energy, to stay aligned with my true self. I'll also connect to the flow of the lifeforce, as it directs me towards all that I want to create.

Trust in the Lifeforce

Just read an excerpt from The Wisdom of Sundays *where Daniel Pink talks about what we'd want our sentence to be.[18] The sentence describing who we were in our life, at the end of it. The key thing is it could only be one sentence. I thought it would be difficult to figure out what mine would*

---

18 Oprah Winfrey, *The Wisdom of Sundays* (Macmillan, 2017)

be. I thought it would take me ages to figure it out. But as soon as I thought about it, it immediately came to me that I'd want it to be:

'She learned how to live from her soul and helped others to do the same.'

I thought, wow, I like that! It feels right and true. It feels like my purpose and my mission to do both.

It feels that my purpose as a human being is the same as every other human being: to live from our souls, to connect with them and listen to the promptings of our souls, and create in the world from them. Whether we are creating a happy home, an amazing business, our best performances as an athlete, meaningful relationships, or being of service to others. Whatever it is that we are each doing, isn't as important as the fact that we are doing it from our soul and drawing the lifeforce into the world as we do.

Whatever we choose to do as an individual will be shaped by our history, personality, character, age, circumstances, life experiences, hobbies, interests, passions. These will all influence how we express the lifeforce in the world, in our unique way. Driven by the promptings of our soul. We need to follow our instincts on what's right for each of us. If we are living from Being and tuned into our soul, our intuition will guide us in what direction to go, towards what is best for each of us.

Putting *Creativity* Into Practice

• You can't cultivate your creativity in your head. You need to cultivate living from Being so that you can dip into the well of creativity that exists within you, in your soul. Make it a priority to work at developing all the other states of Being, and your creative self will certainly emerge.

• Begin recognising where you already express your true self in your daily life, even if you feel you don't, or that you're not connecting with your soul yet. The clues are there, in what makes you feel most yourself, what brings you joy, what you put most of *yourself* into. Start a list of what you begin to notice.

• Write it out. When you are in a calm, centred state and feel that you are connecting with Being, start exploring all that you want to create in the world. Develop it on from what you identified as being what you need. Tune in to the promptings of your soul and go with wherever it takes you in writing it all out. Begin to create the vision of how you and your life will be when you are living from Being, and expressing your creative self. This vision is what you'll develop further in the next chapter, Transformation, and create the framework for you to achieve it. DON'T let your head comment on what goes into your vision, on the practicalities of it, the likelihood of success, what the world will think – don't go there. Look inward and stay out of your head!

- DIVE IN! You can only do it by doing it. If there is a particular way in which you already express your creativity or a way that you would love to, DO IT. For yourself, for creativity itself, to know yourself even more, or just to experience it. Blast any barriers and blocks out of the water by being aware of them, and accept that these are what hold you back, or have in the past. Decide they are not going to do that from now on. Be grateful for knowing what you want to create and that you can do it, and start anywhere, baby steps or bold steps, at your own pace. As you do, be your own supportive creativity coach and friend – we all need one of those.

KEY POINTS: CREATIVITY

- We are all creative Beings, we constantly create the world around us, it is one of our natural states of Being.

- Any vehicle that you use to bring Being into the world is an expression of your creativity.

- Creativity is our growth impulse, driving us to expand our experiences, and imploring us to bring who we are in our souls into alignment with who we are in the world.

- Cultivating your creativity is about opening up to life and allowing it to flood into, and through you, embracing all that it encompasses.

- To feel fulfilled, what you most need is to be completely yourself.

- Being in the creative state of flow is to experience 'the joy of the process of total involvement in life'.

PART III

Experiencing Life as Your Authentic Self

Chapter Nine

Transformation

Transformation is a process of change, which forms its own momentum as it develops. Everything that you do to stay focused and keep going in the same direction builds this momentum and keeps you moving forwards.

By applying yourself to a different course of action from your current one, you initiate the process of transformation. It can be some, or all, of the following: exciting, terrifying, stimulating, uncomfortable, energising, scary, affirming, nerve-wracking, easy, hard work, make you feel vulnerable, a relief, and more. As you can see, it's a mixed bag. You might experience mostly the good stuff, or mostly struggle with the negative aspects of it, or probably a bit of both. It's all part of the process, and the good news is that, if you are *in the process*, you are creating transformation.

Whether you want to experience transformation in only one area of your life, or across the board, the route is the same:

- Figure out what you most want.

- Recognise what you need to change, and how you'll do that.

- Visualise how things are going to be when you have.

- Create a plan to get from A to B, or A to Z!

- Break it into steps and build those into a framework.

- Create a plan of action for incorporating that framework into your life.

- Keep coming back to your plan and your framework, over and over.

Do You Want to Be in a State or in the State of Being?

Transformation is inevitable when you come out of your head and start living more from Being. Creating and experiencing a change in an area of your life, or throughout it, come from the one fundamental change – the shift to prioritising cultivating Being. Then developing a framework, and creating a plan that you can keep realigning with, leads you towards whatever else you want to achieve. This is what helps you stay on track and measure your progress.

Transformation comes from having an array of tools at your disposal that can assist you when there are bumps in the road, or you find yourself lost in the wilderness, wondering how you got there. You can harness the energy of any chaos and destructiveness in your life into creating a plan of what you want to achieve, working out how you're going to achieve it, then following through. You apply yourself to incorporate what you need to into your daily life, and in so doing, redirect your energy into accelerating the process of transformation that coming into Being initiates.

More than likely, you'll feel out of your comfort zone – the known grooves that you have worn into a familiar shape over years and years. No matter how much you want to experience things differently, the old ways of being are a known quantity. Change can feel difficult, scary, or like hard work, but what's the alternative? Continuing to experience what you're already experiencing, at the mercy of your own mind and detached from your soul. To feel that all you want to create is out of reach. To have your attention, and therefore your focus and direction, jump from one concern to the next, in an endless loop. I don't think you'd have got this far in this book if you wanted that.

The decision to live differently takes a second. The fulfilment of that decision takes following through, day by day, step by step, over and over. In cultivating the five states of Being you assemble the building blocks that create a foundation on which to build all that you envision. The next step is to slot these building blocks into a framework to create your own customised blueprint for achieving your vision of all that yourself and your life can be.

Creating YOUR Vision

You did the groundwork for this by creating a list of your wants versus your needs in Gratitude, Chapter 7. Then in Creativity, Chapter 8, you began exploring all that you want to create, in yourself and your world. Now you'll begin to outline your vision by developing these in more detail and depth. If you didn't do those exercises as you read the chapters, do them now. Take time to explore your needs, and what you want to create for yourself and your life. Then you can move on.

If you've used visualisations at all before you'll know that they work best when they are in the present tense, i.e. not 'I am going to be x, and z, or have x, y, and z in my life' but instead, 'I *am* x, y, and z, and I *have* x, y, and z in my life'. The same applies to creating your vision now. You have to imagine all that you want. Then visualise it all *as if you already have it*. With the depth, and type, of feelings, *that you would have if you were already experiencing it all*. Of course, this starts with your imagination.

You want all this to come from your soul, not your head. Yes, you will think about these things in your head, but do it when you are feeling that you are coming from Being. That you are aware, accepting, and in your heart. Do whatever works for you in getting calm and centred, preferably in a quiet place, or at least without distractions. Give yourself the chance to really explore all your vision might be. You want it to resonate with your deepest self. You want it to excite your soul. You might want to start by just doing a brainstorm of what comes up for you. Jotting down words and phrases that seem to capture something of what your vision might contain. Then sink down into yourself and really draw out your deepest desires. Start to build a picture of all that your vision for yourself and your life might contain.

Imagine being that person that you truly are:

- What are you doing?

- How do you feel?

- What is your attitude?

- How do you interact with others?

- What work are you pouring yourself into?

- How do you express yourself from your soul?

- What does your life look like?

- How do you spend your time?

- What are your priorities?

- What are you creating in your world?

Answer these questions. A lot of it might not come to you initially. Stay with it or come back to it over a few days or weeks. Reflect on all of this as you go about your daily life. Come back to here with what you come up with and give yourself the gift of creating your very own vision.

The main thing is to be specific and put as much detail into it as you can. Allow your whole Being to sense it and feel it as if what you imagine is all your experience of life already. This generates a huge amount of energy and motivation and helps you to focus on what you need to do to take you in the direction of fulfilling your vision. You want to really see it. Feel it. Touch it. Taste it. This whets your appetite for achieving it. It all builds belief. It builds determination. It builds will. It sets your intentions.

Don't let your conditioned mind interfere with creating your vision.

It might chirp in often. With why you can't do this or that. With why and how you'll fail. It'll remind you of all the things you've failed at in the past. It will ridicule your dreams, laugh at you. Tell you you're stupid for daring to believe that you can achieve your deepest desires. It will also keep pulling you away from the creation of your vision because your vision is generated from Being. As you now know, your head wants to create you and your world – from *its* dictates. It wants control. It wants to allow all your fears, neuroses, destructive habits, and emotional turmoil to be what creates your world. That's the way it's been to date. That's what it knows. That's how it keeps control. Don't let it.

Last, or actually, first, to be your true self, to recognise your own soul, and be guided by it, in achieving all that you want to achieve, the first part of your vision has to be about coming into Being. That is what this book is about. Coming into Being, and living from it, is the first thing you need to work on, to create all else that you want to create. It has to be a fundamental part of your vision. You waken up to the grip your mind has had on you, come out of your head and into your heart, then you begin cultivating awareness and acceptance, and discover your true wants and needs. You are then able to truly know what the rest of your vision contains because it'll come from your authentic self.

My Vision of Being

When I first created my vision in the way that I've just described, it was mostly about how I'd be feeling, and living, by following the steps to cultivate living *in* Being. Alongside that were some health and wellbeing considerations, and what I most wanted for my relationships. You'll see all that it was comprised of in my framework (below). I worked with this vision for a while. As I started to live more in Being and began fulfilling that vision, I created a second vision for what I wanted to create *from* Being. This book is the partial fulfilment of that second vision, and I'm still focusing on creating much of it.

Then after months and months of beginning to make some headway in feeling that I was living more from this vision, I began to create mini visions for different areas of my life. I would then add the steps to achieving them into my framework. For instance, a specific one about what I wanted to create with my writing, then one about how I wanted my closest relationships to be different. In the past two or three years I've revisited my vision roughly every six months or so, and really just added on more specific goals of what I want to create and how I'll do it. I feel that it clarifies my intentions, gets them more specific and detailed, which in turn helps me keep on track with how I want to live my life.

I refer back to it often. It keeps me on track with the foundation of what I still want to create. It also reminds me of how far I've come since I first wrote it.

I still have to keep myself on track with my initial vision, even while I work towards newer ones. It's something I put myself into achieving daily. Some days are more successful than others! It reminds me to keep coming back to Being, over and over. That it is the foundation of everything else that I want to create.

My Framework

As detailed previously, I've worked as a counsellor/therapist, had personal counselling, and read countless books on self-development. I gained insight and understanding as I explored many concepts and learned a lot about myself. What I didn't feel I had developed was a practical way to build all of this into my daily life. I began to realise that the more structure I could put around what felt instinctively to be the right path, around my vision, the easier it would be to become my default – an automatic habit.

I realised that in developing the food business that I co-founded, I had similarly developed a vision for what I wanted it to become. But then I had also created a strategy of all the different elements that I would need to work on to make that vision a reality. I then broke all of those elements down into what I'd need to do daily/weekly/monthly to stay on track. Why wasn't I doing the same when it came to my own personal development and my spiritual growth?

It's great to have a vision of what you want to experience and create, even better to have it vividly documented. It's very inspiring and motivating. For years I had done something similar in working out what my goals were and imagining and detailing them. The difference this time was twofold. First, the vision was more vividly imagined, more detailed, and backed by the emotional intensity of imagining having already achieved the vision. Imagining how I'd feel when I'd created all that I wanted to as if it had already happened. Second, as in my business, I deconstructed my vision and pulled out the key elements. Then I further broke those down into practical steps to include in my life day by day, to achieve each of these elements. All of this then became my framework for creating my vision. I would refer to it often. It made it easier to keep on track. The process is detailed below.

Over time, I've added different tools to the basic framework, that helped me to stay on track. I've detailed these ideas also. They've worked for me – some better than others. You can try whichever you feel might be best for you or try them all. As most of them are about cultivating living more in and from Being, then your initial vision might look remarkably similar to this, or you can just use this as your base framework. Then later, add your own ideas for what could help *you* stay on track.

The Elements of My Framework

1. Living in Being (love, awareness, acceptance, gratitude, and creativity)

2. Health and wellbeing

3. Relationships

4. Self-concept

5. Work (creativity/lifeforce)

6. Gratitude

7. The bigger picture (adventures, passions, fun, the fullness of life)

Practical Daily Steps

The following is how I incorporated these different elements into my life, to stay aligned with my vision.

1. Living in Being

Awareness – noticing my thoughts as they cascade through my mind. Noticing my emotions as they bubble up.

Love – as I go about my day, often noticing whether I am in my head or in my heart. Bring my awareness, my attention, back to residing in my heart. When I want to think through things, come back to my heart, to a place of awareness, acceptance, peace, and love, first.

Acceptance – not judging or criticising myself for whatever I notice. Accepting what is. Allowing *what is* to just be. Letting my thoughts and emotions go, as they are replaced by other thoughts and emotions, that again, I just notice.

Gratitude – bringing my attention often to all that I have. Appreciate my good fortune. Whenever I notice that I'm complaining to myself in my head, or to others, pull my attention towards all that I am, and have. Keep whatever I'm complaining about in perspective by remembering all that I have to be grateful for from the most fundamental needs of food, shelter, and relationships, to health, to my abilities, to how I spend my time, to my material possessions.

* * *

As I did, you can help yourself stay on track with all of the above elements of your own vision related to coming more into Being, by tying them to certain situations/activities.

Sticky notes in your bedroom – on your mirror, on your bedside table, on a photo frame next to where you get dressed – just saying 'notice'. That starts the process that leads into acceptance, with notes saying 'head to heart' folded in your purse, stuck to the back of your phone, or on your car steering wheel – anywhere! Make a mental note that when you make a cup of tea or wash pots, to notice your thoughts and feelings and come into awareness. Then bring your attention from your head to your heart. This links whatever the activity you are doing with becoming more aware, more present, and coming out of your head and into your heart.

> The more activities you link to coming
> into Being, the easier it will be to remember
> to do it, to set the process in motion,
> over and over.

2. Health and Wellbeing

For me, this was broken down into becoming slimmer and leaner, eating healthily, and feeling calmer and more centred, so my plan looked as follows:

- Eat fewer sugar-laden, processed, and generally 'unhealthy' foods. Eat more lightly by having more soup, salads, veg, lean protein, plus lower-sugar and wholegrain snacks. Only eat biscuits or cake moderately, and when I do, enjoy and appreciate them. Drink lots of water. Drink less alcohol and only socially.

- Be conscious of my food choices. Make choices aligned with the vision I want to create.

- Walk for a minimum of half an hour, at least five days a week. Do yoga, either classes or at home.

- Meditate for twenty minutes each day.

- Carve out time to build these activities into my life as often as possible, to build up to the ideal of doing them most days.

3. Relationships

Prioritise nurturing the relationships that are important to me. Make time for the people I love. *Really* listen to them. Accept them for who they are, faults and all, and accept whatever stage of their journey they are at in life. Consciously come out of my head and into my heart when I am interacting with others. Notice my own internal responses to them. Instead of acting from the judgements, irritations, criticisms, frustrations, that come up, just notice them. Then come into my heart, remind myself of the love I have for them, and act from the love in my heart.

4. Self-concept

Remind myself daily that who I truly am is not who I see in the mirror. I'm not the clothes I wear. I'm not the stories of my life. Not the labels that society has given me. I'm not who others relate to me as – not the collection of my old habits and behaviours. Remind myself daily that who I truly am is a spiritual being. Living in, and creating from, a state of Being. From love. From my grateful heart. *This* is who I am. *This* is how I see myself. Every day I bring myself back to this self-concept. Every time I look in the mirror, I remind myself of it. I rest in it throughout the day.

5. Work (creativity/lifeforce)

Whatever work I'm doing, I put my true self into it. As I work, I remind myself to notice whether I am in my head or my heart. If I'm in my head, I pause, take a few moments to focus on my breathing, become aware, and draw the centre of my attention, my awareness, back down to my heart. I come into Being over and over and create from that place. I keep coming into Being. As I do, I realign myself with the flow of the lifeforce. I draw it through me and put it out into the world. I notice the voice of my soul in the ideas, promptings, and urges that come to me. I stay in my heart and follow them. Letting them lead me to all that I am meant to Be and create.

6. Gratitude

Every day I pause regularly to appreciate all that I have. When I'm drinking a cup of tea. When I first sit down in my favourite chair. When I'm drinking a glass of water. I tie as many of my daily activities as possible to cultivating a grateful heart. I re-read the first few pages of my gratitude journal, of all the fundamental and constant things that I am grateful for. I regularly write down, or acknowledge verbally, or in my head, the little things that I appreciate every day.

7. The Bigger Picture

Every day I remind myself of how fragile, finite, and precious life is. I remind myself to let go of ruminating on the minutiae of day-to-day existence. I hold this in my awareness as I go about my day. I make time to stop and smell the roses. I carve out time for adventures and follow my soul in what these can be. I also shift my perspective on what adventure is, and find fun and joy in daily life. I realise how important this is in living a full, fulfilled, and happy life. Most mornings, I re-read my vision, or listen to the recording of it as I walk, or as I drive, or I re-read these steps.

Most evenings, either before bed, or as I fall asleep, I evoke the feelings of having my vision fulfilled. I rest in them. I build the depth and clarity of how it feels having created all that I wanted to create, into every cell of my body. I give thanks for it, and let the peace and joy from experiencing it flow over me.

* * *

Did I, or do I, do all of the above every day? No. Have I ever done all of the above for a full day? Probably not. Do I do some of the above most days? Yes. Do I ever feel that I'm *living* the vision that I first captured many, many months ago? Often.

It took me a while to introduce all the aspects of the practical steps. For instance, before I created my vision, I had already been walking most days for half an hour to keep fit and lose weight. I was also eating healthily as much as possible. I had also meditated on and off at various times over the years but had never built it into a daily practice. I decided to try to do it most days for twenty minutes and as early in the morning as possible. Again, I had done yoga in classes a few times but not for a while, so I did a couple of classes again and then started aiming do twenty minutes of yoga four or five times a week at home. It took me a few months to establish my meditation practice before I introduced yoga.

So, as you can see, I wasn't going from a standing start when I created my vision and the framework by which to make it a reality. In pulling together all of the elements of my vision, I was looking at what I was already working towards creating, and building on that further, to incorporate all of what felt important for me. I knew the steps had to be ones that I could incorporate into my life, and that I wouldn't be likely to do them all at once.

Your vision and your practical steps to creating it are evolving things. They are meant to be inspiring and supportive, and help draw you towards, and keep on track for, achieving all that you want to create in *your* vision.

Your vision is *not* a set of rules that you beat yourself up about 'breaking'; they are not all or nothing. They are not meant, or likely to, be followed by you, to the letter, from day one.

Obviously, the more of the practical steps you can do every day, the sooner you are likely to experience the beginning of a transformation in yourself and your life. Your vision and framework are *ideals* – what you aspire to. What you are envisioning into being. They are what you want to experience, and a roadmap of how you can get there. They are for clarity, direction, and focus, *to help you.* Not to hold you to account or make you feel bad about yourself for not doing them.

Even if you start with baby steps, and gradually build the different elements of your vision into your life through the practical steps, as I did, you will be going in the right direction, and be clearer about what you want to create. You will be moving away from all that you don't want, towards what you do. You will be choosing to step out of the old, ingrained patterns of thoughts and behaviours that take away from, rather than add anything to, your life. You'll be turning away from these patterns that have taken you to where you don't want to be, experiencing what you don't want to be experiencing.

Try to do something from the practical steps every day and encourage yourself to do as many of them as you can manage, at any given time. Then build on them, day by day, step by step. Remember, transformation doesn't happen by the wave of a magic wand or during your sleep one night. It happens as you lay one building block on top of another, over and over, in the actions that you take every day. Before you know it, you realise you are experiencing more and more of your vision. It feels fantastic. It feels well worth all the effort, the sacrifices, the application, and the determination and courage you've had to generate.

Toolkit

These are a collection of tools that I've used at various times to help me in putting my framework into practice. They have helped me stay on track with creating my vision. You may have other ideas (let me know about them if you do!). Some of these tools might not feel as if they would be helpful for you. Go with your instincts – maybe give at least some of them a try before discounting them. These are just what has felt helpful to me.

List of Key Phrases from Your Vision

This is helpful when you don't have enough time to read over, or listen to, your whole vision but want to be kept on track by its essence. This is a shorthand reminder of the elements that your vision contains.

Practical Daily Steps

As I just described above, although you'll want to fine-tune each of these actions to fit with your own needs and daily schedules.

Daily Plan

From those overriding practical steps, you can break it down further into a timetable of actions to do each day (or as many as possible, most days) to stay aligned with your vision and set reminders to prompt you to be 'aware' or 'grateful', for example. Mine looked like this:

Daily Plan

Morning

- Healthy breakfast
- Read or listen to my vision
- Meditate
- Work – have awareness/acceptance/gratitude/head-to-heart reminders around me

After Lunch

- Work (as above)
- Thirty-minute walk – while catching up on phone calls, or listening to recordings of reminders, or a spiritual podcast

After Dinner

- Family time
- Reading/downtime
- Visualisation of feelings of a vision fulfilled before bed

Throughout the Day (Reminders)

- Awareness and acceptance
- Head to heart
- Gratitude

Self-questioning

I love firing questions at myself! Even though it's you, asking yourself them, you'll be surprised by some of the answers. Often, I'll gain valuable insight or understanding from it. Not just with coming to live in and from Being. I might just feel unsure of what's going on for me or have an issue or area of my life that I feel stuck with. I'll ask myself the questions that might give me a nudge in the right direction. Like you would if you were trying to help a friend get a handle on something in their life that they were wrestling with.

If you're just re-reading your vision or elements of your framework, or practical steps, over and over, it can feel a bit repetitive, and/or lose some of its impact. It's good to change your approach some days. Instead of, or as well as, reading them, ask yourself some questions that remind you of the essence of all that you are trying to achieve. These are some of the questions I might ask myself, but you might have others that you feel would work better for you:

- Am I in my head or my heart NOW?

- Which me do I want to be – Head Me or Heart Me?

- Which would help me most in this moment/ situation?

- Who would I be now if I was living from my heart? What would I be doing?

- Am I kind to myself and others? Am I in my heart as I connect with them?

- How can I make the most of my time and myself now?

- Can I sense Being within me? Do I want to live from here?

- What do I need to be doing in this moment that would help keep me on track?

- How can I make the most of my time and myself here and now?

- Can I Be rather than do? Can I Be as I do?

- What can I find to *love* about where I am and what I am doing?

- What do I appreciate today? What am I grateful for?

- Am I accepting myself? Am I accepting my current situation and circumstances?

- How am I treating my body today? Am I prioritising my health and my mental and emotional wellbeing?

- Am I putting *myself* into whatever I'm doing today – my *true* self?

- Am I staying open to allowing the lifeforce to flow through me into my life?

- Am I allowing myself to be guided by the inspiration and promptings of my soul?

- Do I remember the bigger picture of life?

- Am I making time for appreciating the fullness of life, for curiosity, adventure, or fun?

Quotes

It might be your old favourite ones, or it might be some that you find throughout this book. It might just be an extract of a sentence or a few lines, that speaks to you. I have a little notebook in which I've written my favourites over the years. I remind myself to pull it out when I want to be inspired, comforted, or reminded of what I had forgotten. There are also lots of mini books of quotes, either general or on specific topics that you can get to dip in and out of.

Settling Down Inside Yourself

Sometimes, you might feel distracted by external circumstances, or the contents of your own mind (I call it being in 'twirly mind'!). Often, it's because life has gotten busy, a lot is going on, or too many diverse things are vying for your attention. This is the time you are most likely to revert to old, ingrained patterns of thoughts and behaviours. The key is recognising this state and then knowing how to bring yourself back to a calm, centred state. My technique for dealing with this, which you might like to try, is as follows:

1. Find a quiet place where you can be on your own for ten minutes. If not, then do it as best you can wherever you are, and whatever you're doing.

2. Start by putting your attention on your breathing, dragging it from whatever your mind is absorbed in, letting go of the need to think.

3. Consciously slow your breathing down, pausing after the out-breath. Imagine relaxation sliding down from your head and through your whole body.

4. As you do this, begin some soothing self-talk. For example, you might say: 'It's OK to let go. You can go back to what you were thinking about later, but for now, you don't need to think. You don't need to think about anything right now. You don't need to figure anything out right now. You're OK. Everything is OK. Let go. Let go. Let go.'

5. Keep going until you feel an internal shift: your mind slowing and quietening.

6. Try to feel the sensation of coming back into your body from your head – of settling down inside yourself.

When I do feel that, I usually sigh with relief that I've escaped the clutches of 'twirly mind', and I start to feel calm and centred again.

Truth, Choices, Consequences, Alternatives

If you go off the rails in sticking to your intentions, as I often did, you may feel disheartened, down, or a bit lost. When this happened to me, I would alternate between beating myself up for not following through with my plans or trying to justify to myself having fallen back into old, familiar habits. Until I realised that, at these times, I hadn't been telling myself the truth.

If this happens, the first step is to be truthful about why you've wandered off track, which is where this Truth, Choices, Consequences, Alternatives exercise can be helpful:

1. Be honest with yourself about why you've wandered off track.

2. Remember the sequence of events (what had been going on mentally and emotionally leading up to you slipping into old patterns of behaviour?).

3. Look at the choices you made at each stage of the way and the consequences that those choices have created.

4. Finally, reflect on the different choices you could have made at each stage, and what would have been the consequences of those.

When I do this exercise, I write it all out in bullet points. In the overview of it all, I can then see more clearly what happened, why it has, and what lessons I could learn to do something differently next time. Instead of just feeling bad about yourself or pushing it all out of your mind and trying to get back on the rails without learning anything for next time, this process helps you be proactive in dealing with it and will help you stay truer to your vision in the future. This is a handy tool that I'd urge you to try.

I often remind myself to do this exercise. It doesn't need to take long. You're just trying to capture the essence of what happens at these times, the key points, to get a different perspective on things.

Aligned Actions/Non-aligned Actions

When you have a vision of what is most vital for you to create, then you can start to prioritise how you spend your time. Creating the life you want isn't about what you do in the future, it's about what you do now, each day. The choices you make about how you spend your time, either take you towards what you need and want, or press the pause button on you moving towards it.

For this one, you may like to write a list of what things you can do that will most keep you travelling in the direction of your vision. I call this my list of Aligned Actions. I go back to it often, and add things, or take away things from it. It's a shorthand for keeping me on track. At any time, you can give yourself a 'stop and think' by saying, 'Is how I'm spending my time now an Aligned Action?' Then you'll know if you're following through on your plans or not. This is also helpful if you're feeling a bit lost, or lacking motivation. You can look at the list and do any Aligned Action to start the process of getting back on track.

When you've done this, think about when you spend your time and energy on things that don't take you towards what you most want, or don't help you in being fully yourself. These are your Non-aligned Actions. You've now got a clear distinction between the things that you need to do less of, and those you need to do more of – to take yourself in the direction that you want to go.

Part of this is figuring out the things which help you to stay connected to and be, and express, your authentic self. For me, I've come to realise that I lose myself when I get locked in my head, with the paralysis of overthinking, or if I choose to overindulge in food, alcohol, or screens, too often. These choices take me away from being myself. I lose my connection to my true self. I press the pause button on the life I want to create. On the other hand, in choosing to direct myself towards one of my Aligned Actions, I find myself again.

Writing It Out

I often find my way through difficulties by writing it all out. I don't think this is just because I'm a writer. Often people will draw up a pros and cons list if they need to make a decision, or write a letter to someone that they don't post, to be clearer about how they feel, or just to get it all out.

As well as a journal, I have a notebook that I often just write it all out in. I get the jumbled contents of my mind down on paper. Then immediately, or after I've re-read it, I tear out the pages, rip them up, and throw them away. I find it cathartic. It's a release, and it gets things out of my head, as well as helping me to see more clearly what is going on for me. If you want to try it, you don't need to think about what you want to write. Just start writing, ask yourself questions if you want, as a prompt, and just write, and write, and write it all out.

Word Wall

Similarly to Writing It Out, if you don't have the time, the inclination, or energy, to write screeds, or just want to regroup and sense where you are with things, just write down the words that best capture what's going on for you at the time. I mix it up with capital letters, words at a slant, underline some, or use different-coloured pens. Then I just reflect on it, as if it's a picture. It's a brainstorm of where I am and what's going on. A snapshot of it. A psychological dump. Somehow capturing it like that helps.

Daily Word

Think of what feels most important to remember, feel, Be, do, or focus on *that day*. Ponder on the word that would best help you with that. Then use that word as a kind of mantra for the day, or sometimes for a few days or even a week. Bring it to mind often, and it can serve as a shortcut to remembering what is most important for you that day. For me, it becomes my focus for the day, an easy reminder of an aspect of my vision that I most want to pay attention to. It could be 'intention', 'determination', 'stillness', 'love', or whatever feels right for you with what's going on for you at the time, and/or what word would most help you stay on track.

Daily Points Tally

Sometimes when you look back on your day or week, you might find it hard to judge how well you've stuck to your plans. You can give yourself a kind of points system for the practical steps of your daily plan. For me, I'd award a point for doing yoga, eating healthily, meditating, etc. I'd tot them up at the end of the day to see how many out of the actions I'd completed. If I'd achieved anywhere between five and eight points, I was still on track; between three and five and I'd try to do better the next day; but a one or two, and I'd need to have a talk to myself! If you try this tally system, write the number in your diary or calendar each day, as a record of how you are doing weekly or monthly.

Remember, Remember, Remember

Creating a series of reminders linked to your daily activities is one of the best ways to stay on track with creating your vision. These reminders might be the list of bullet points of the elements of your vision, or the practical steps, on index cards or pieces of paper, or in a note on your phone. You might want to, as I did, read your vision aloud and record it for yourself, then have it on your phone. Then if you're out walking, or working, or doing anything where you can stick in your earphones and listen to it, you have it handy. You're reinforcing all that you want to create, to let it drive your actions. As I mentioned before, you can also link reminders to activities you do every day, like brushing your teeth, making a cup of coffee, getting dressed, etc.

Reminders are so important because they help you to establish new routines, and the more you consciously do them and build them into your day, the sooner they will become more automatic. You won't even need to remind yourself to do them.

Pep Talks

Have a pep talk ready for yourself as soon as you start the process of working towards your vision. Have it prepared for when you're ready to throw in the towel on your efforts, or on days when you forget where you're going, or why you want to do what you're doing. Maybe you don't have the energy, time, or inclination, to start re-reading your vision and framework. Have a short list of bullet points, or a few phrases, written down: a reminder of why you want to stay on track, and all that is to be gained from it. Keep it to hand and use it to recharge your enthusiasm, and strengthen your courage and commitment to staying on track.

* * *

That's it for the toolkit. I'm sure you'll also have, or find, many of your own ways to help you achieve the fulfilment of your vision. The main thing is to use them and regularly. Build them into your life to support you in doing what you want to do.

Creating YOUR Framework

Having created your vision and seen all the elements of my framework that you can draw on, you can now create your own. Think of it as a blueprint for building your vision; it's all the practical steps, in a structure that you can work through, bit by bit. If you just focus on the vision and don't create a framework, you may find a chasm opens up in the space between where you are now and living the life you envision. Without a structure in place, your vision can pull you forward so far, but at the first bumps in the road, you end up thrown off course, lost in the woods, not knowing how to get back on track.

Alternatively, with a structure in place, you are breaking down the journey into more manageable stages. All along the way, you know what you need to do to get to the next stage. If you go off track, you only need to refer to your framework to know the steps you need to take to get back on it again. That makes it a lot easier. Neville

Goddard talks about 'faithful, systematic, cultivation of the vision fulfilled'.[19] I love that! It says it all in how to achieve a vision.

Faithful: The process just rolls along and works if you believe in the power of the lifeforce flowing through you, and connect to it through living from Being, and have faith in yourself.

Systematic: Your framework contains a system of components, customised to suit you, that together, followed step by step, lead you to your own personal transformation.

Cultivation: Working at it, being patient, doing what's necessary, nurturing yourself and your growth, and helping yourself to stay on track.

Vision fulfilled: Having a vision, creating it, drawing yourself towards it with all that you do. Growing into it, *fulfilling* it, and in doing so, fulfilling your unique potential as a human being.

You are now ready to do all of the above and start detailing the elements of your own framework. Try different things, see what works for you. It doesn't have to be something you complete in one session and have it all set out. Great if you want to, and feel ready to, but it can also be constructed over a period of time, as you work out what elements you need to incorporate into the framework to best suit you and your vision. However you do it, as you do, keep your vision alive and vivid in your whole being.

At a later date, you'll probably want to rewrite parts of your framework, as you find out by trial and error what is

---

19 Neville Goddard, *The Power of Awareness* (G. & J. Publishing Co., 1952)

manageable for you, and how much you feel you're moving towards your vision. As I mentioned before, I've created visions for different aspects of my life, as well as the overall one, and add to my framework, or edit it, each time I do. Your framework will evolve and develop and change as you do. Remember, it's not something to beat yourself over the head with. It's a positive, proactive, support tool. It's your best friend on the road to cultivating living from Being and experiencing all that you want your life to be.

A Spiritual Practice

I used to think that spiritual practice was meditating or praying. But *anything* that you do regularly, that brings you back into Being, is a spiritual practice. Anything in your routines that connects you to the spiritual Being that you are is a spiritual practice. Working on awareness and acceptance are spiritual practices, as is consciously coming out of your head and into your heart.

> *Any* way in which you repeatedly bring
> yourself back to Being becomes
> your spiritual practice.

The more in your vision and framework that keeps you on track with living in and from Being that you do regularly, the more you'll grow and strengthen Being within you. Building spiritual practices into your daily life are what connects you with Being.

Follow Your Intentions, Not Your Urges

As you work through cultivating a new way of Being, you will likely have to drag yourself out of your comfort zone. You are also likely to encounter internal resistance because we don't like feeling uncomfortable. Your usual way of operating in the world is your default setting, and you're trying to reprogramme yourself to new settings. When you encounter these obstacles of resistance on the road, you may feel like you lack the psychological or emotional energy or strength to overcome them. The answer is to have a shortcut at the ready. A great big arrow to point you back on track. That shortcut is your intentions.

Intentions are what you *intend* to do. They are the clearest expression of your forward trajectory; they are the *why* and the *how* of your vision and framework. Your intentions are a promise to yourself that you will do what you have to do, to fulfil the desires of your deepest, truest self, of your soul.

Why?

Because you can see the rewards of getting to where you want to Be.

How?

You know how to do it, it's not complicated, you've created a plan, and you know that all you need to do is take those steps, repeatedly.

No matter how you are feeling, whatever curveballs life throws at you, however tired, demotivated, hopeless, or full of doubt you are – you can follow your intentions instead of your urges.

Your urges might be fleeting, and ever-changing, or they may be persistent and repetitive. And they may feel powerful and overwhelming. They are generated from who you've been, and how you've lived your life, in the past. They are urges to continue in habits and behaviours that no longer serve you, and that won't help you in creating your vision. Your intentions, on the other hand, come from the core of who you are, where your power and strength lie. They pull you towards all that you want to be, living the life that you want to live. Draw on this power and strength to stick to your intentions. Again, be your own best friend in encouraging yourself to stay on track with what you intend to do.

Creating Your Intentions

Write down your intentions. You don't have to write pages, it can just be a few sentences or a bullet point list of the whys of what you intend to create for yourself. Think about the commitments you are making to yourself to create all that you want and the reasons for doing it. Boil it down to your key priorities for this stage on your journey. These commitments and priorities create your intentions. They are what is most important to you.

When you have a clear idea of your intentions, remind yourself of them often. Keep them close to your heart, ready to engage them in the service of keeping you on course. Your intentions become the energy that you put out into the world.

Your intentions create all
that you experience.

Choice, Choice, Choice

Underlying this whole process is the fact that everything hangs on the choices we make in each moment of every day. Big choices and decisions play their part, but it is our tiny choices, the ones we're usually barely conscious of, which accumulate to shape our lives and create what we experience. Often, we don't *think* we're actively choosing how to behave or what we think and feel, but you can see by now that we always have the choice where to put our attention. It's just that a lot of how we are, and what we do, has gone onto automatic pilot, and we merely exist from our default settings.

You'll become aware of the choices you make in what you think, how you feel, and in your behaviours. Who you interact with, and how. How you choose to live day to day. When you do this, you'll realise more and more, that as you do, you are also choosing what you experience in life. Coming more into Being and cultivating awareness and acceptance of the choices you make is the first step to choosing differently.

You've created a vision for how you would like your life to be, and how you'd be living it. Every choice you make, in every moment, either takes you towards that vision or not. Staying aware of this is another good shortcut to keeping you on track. Rather than having to think through why you do, or don't, want to be doing a certain thing. Ask yourself the simple question: does this move me in the direction of my vision? That's how you stay on track with your vision in *all* that you do. You then develop an automatic *knowing*, whether or not something is right for you. Whether or not you are staying on track in your thoughts and actions.

Be determined to repeatedly make the choices that
draw you forward to all that you most want.
This becomes a lot easier, the more that
you do it, and the more you live in,
and from, Being.

Taking Responsibility for Your Choices

Be honest with yourself. Don't kid yourself on that
the choices you make are because of other people or
circumstances. No matter what you're dealing with, or
how ingrained it is, how hard it feels to change, or how a
circumstance or situation might seem like somebody else's
'fault', you almost always have the responsibility for most of
your choices. You have the opportunity to make choices for
health, creativity, growth, and forward progress, instead of
choosing escape, anaesthesia, avoidance, distraction, or
comfort.

Don't let yourself off the hook, and that doesn't mean
beating yourself up about making the wrong choices. It
just means looking at the choices you make with clear
eyes. Being honest with yourself. Realising that you
could have made other choices and making an honest
commitment to yourself that you will next time. Then
move on, don't ruminate on the wrong choices – focus on
where you want to go, and the choices that will take you
there.

What's the Alternative?

Sometimes, it might seem like too gargantuan an effort to get yourself back on the rails. You might feel you just don't have the time, energy, or inclination. It might feel like too difficult a task. You might defeatedly wonder why you should bother, as you'll probably just end up off the rails again at some point anyway. What's the alternative though? To revert back to your default settings. To forget about trying to become who you truly are, or trying to create the life you most want. That's an option.

You'll be back to experiencing all that you experienced before. It may be less challenging than trying to push towards your vision. You'll be back in your comfort zone, and that might feel good for a bit, even if you're not that happy there, you're *comfortable*. Or, it may feel even worse, because you'll have lost the hope that things could be different. You'll have lost your dream of the vision for yourself and your life.

At these times, more than ever, be honest with yourself about what you want, and what you are willing to do to get there. Remind yourself of your vision, re-read your intentions, remind yourself of what coming to live more in, and from, Being brings. Remind yourself of what you want to experience in your life, and how that might feel.

Remind yourself of all this not to persuade yourself to try again, but to honestly look at what you want to turn your back on. Do what you need to do to come into Being and know in your soul whether you want to abandon the chance to be fulfilling your unique potential as a human being by living from Being. Then, it's your choice. When it comes to this journey, you only have yourself to answer to.

Journal:
The Road of Change

These journal extracts are about my realisations of the transformational aspects of coming to live in, and from, Being.

Be Honest

Be honest with myself. Stop telling myself stories. Stop kidding myself. Stop buying into the inane chatter in my mind. Stick to the facts. The thought patterns: notice them, accept them, let go of them, choose to come back to Being.

Choose Being, choose wellness, choose the life I want to live, choice by choice, every day, day after day; put in the hours, do what I need to do to create what I want to create. Simple.

A Reminder to Myself

What does it mean to live, love, and create in Being? It means residing in the spiritual being that I am. Inhabiting my Being rather than my head. It means that from a place of awareness, I'm aligned with who I truly am. It means that when I make decisions or act from that place, I will be taking myself and my life in the direction I want to go. It means that I choose not to follow the urges, compulsions, and automatic ingrained patterns of my conditioned self. They have not served me well and take me away from who I want to be, and how I want to live my life.

Recognising the difference between the two and noticing where I am before acting, allows me to choose to act from

Being. To take the actions aligned with creating the life I want for myself. Whether it's about what I'm doing, how I'm interacting, or in my choices around food and alcohol.

A few days later . . .

I can already feel the power of doing the above, and I've only been doing it sporadically. My visualisations are going to be about making this a habitual way of living. I'm getting better at noticing when I'm not in Being and pulling myself back to it.

To BE List

It occurred to me that rather than my priority being my TO DO list, it should be my TO BE list! I have to make it a priority to be aware, to be present, to be living consciously if I really want to create a different way of living my life.

I have to make time for things that help me to do that. I have to have a structure for them and plan them. Otherwise, I'm busy doing, and making time for doing, and not remembering what brings me to just Be, what helps facilitate Being.

Choices

It's all about the choices I make in the moment. Minute-by-minute choices that take me towards the way I want to be living my life and the person I want to be, or don't. Choices of what I focus on, where I put my attention, mentally or emotionally, whether or not I'm applying myself to my priorities; how to be, how to behave, how to act, when to act or not. Conscious choices.

Be aware of my choices. Slow down and notice the choices I have at any time, and make the choices aligned with my vision for my life and myself. Choices to be the best me that I can be, to focus on my priorities and in doing so, fulfilling my potential as a human being.

My List

I've written this list before, probably many times. I want to write it again. To remind me, and as an outflowing of what I need for forward motion, for growth.

They are the building blocks that I just need to do as many of as I can every day to create what I want to create – to create the life I want to be living. Consistently and persistently, I need to build them into my life. These actions keep me aligned with all that I most want to create for myself and in my life.

- *Live consciously, keep bringing myself back to Being*

- *Awareness: here and now, noticing over and over*

- *Accepting what I see in awareness*

- *Eating lightly, healthily, and nourishingly*

- *Drink lots of water*

- *Minimum sugar and alcohol – a balance, not excess*

- *Walking*

- *Writing*

- *Reading*

- *Meditation*

- *Yoga*

- *Choosing to be happy and at peace*

- *Plenty of sleep*

- *Carve out time for silence and solitude*

Re-connecting to My Vision

Feeling good in my own skin. Just back from a great yoga class, and I can feel my body beginning to change. The strong, lean body buried under all the fat is emerging bit by bit. The limp muscle is toning up and beginning to become more noticeably toned.

Earlier today, for the first time in a month, I had a feeling of wanting to give up. I wanted to forget yoga tonight, eat lots, and have lots of alcohol. It felt like an automatic reflex response to how I've been feeling for the past few days – a bit demotivated, tired, lethargic, low – that probably got me into that frame of mind. I realised that coinciding with feeling that way, or maybe due to it, I haven't been reading my journal and vision. I have lost touch with what I wanted and my vision of it.

I re-read the first entry of my journal where I'd written what I want to create and how I was going to get there, and it re-inspired me. I felt that I wanted to go to yoga again and although I still felt a bit lacking in energy, I didn't want to go completely off the rails and do the opposite of all that I really wanted for myself. I went to yoga, enjoyed it, had a quiet night afterwards and ate a big healthy dinner and went to bed early. I cared for myself instead of abusing myself with excess food and alcohol.

It reminded me of the importance of reminding myself daily of what I want, of the vision that I want to create. It definitely helps pull you towards it.

The Power of a Quote

Hungover. Feeling fuzzy-headed and lacking in focus. A bit negative. A bit tired. Feeling rudderless. I felt the day slipping away. I needed something to help me get centred and know that all is good.

I felt that I needed some time to go through my writings or read or write. To find something to help me get back on track. Then I went to the back of my notebook and read a couple of Eckhart Tolle quotes.

The second one I read immediately brought me back to Being. I instantly felt totally aware and at peace, and it felt miraculous. My mood shifted hugely. I felt aware, present, at peace, and full of joy. The quote was: 'Sense within you an unconditioned, timeless consciousness that is nothing to do with thinking.'[20]

On another day, with a different set of circumstances and/ or feelings, it might not have the same effect, and maybe another quote would, but for today that worked, and it was wonderful.

---

20 Eckhart Tolle, *The Power of Now* (Hodder & Stoughton, 2001)

Routes to My Soul

It's clear to me that there are many different routes to knowing who you are. Sometimes just awareness is enough for me. Noticing my thoughts or mental patterns, or my emotional states can be enough to bring me to my core, my soul, because I realise that it is my true self that is doing the noticing. That awareness is my true self.

Sometimes it's appreciating all that I have, and all that I am, or other people. Sometimes it's feeling love for, or connection to, others that bring me to feeling connected to my own soul. At other times I actively seek out the connection by practising mindfulness or meditating, to take me to the stillness within me.

All of these are routes to my soul, and there are many more. All of these help me to stay connected to who I truly am. The lifeforce. To knowing it, trusting in it, let myself be guided by it. The more routes I have to stay connected, the more likely I am to be living from that place. The more I do that, the more I will be aligned with the desires of my soul and create them in the world.

I and Me

I've been finding it hard to get any silence and solitude. Lots going on around about me for weeks. I was getting really tense and unhappy about it because I felt that I was really craving it. It felt really important to have it, and I felt that I could get no peace.

Then, while feeling tense and unhappy, I could suddenly clearly see the 'me' that was craving it. I could see how much my mind was attaching certain conditions to me being able to find peace and happiness. That I should be on my own, in silence, and for a while.

I thought about the 'I' that could see what the 'me' was doing, and how I was creating my own unhappiness by chasing something – some ideal set of conditions for peace and happiness.

When I saw that, I felt instant happiness and peace. I came to rest in the 'I' that could see the pain and frustration caused by the desires and dictates of my head (me, me, me). I felt a strong sense of the underlying force, waiting there for me, where I could rest anytime, no matter what was going on around me.

It feels much easier to go there now because I had such a powerful and real experience of it. It's not a mental concept that I can think my way into. I just need to let go of the mental concepts that go with Head Me. Then I'm instantly 'I' – an aware presence, living in peace, joy, and contentment – Being. Feeling total acceptance and understanding, going with the flow of life.

I'm reflecting on what reminders I could have for myself on the differences between Head Me and 'I' – Being. An interesting idea popped into my head.

'I' is for intuition, instinct, intelligence, illumination, imagination, innocence, immense, immediate, infinite, insight, inspiration, integrity, intension, intimacy, invention/ innovation. . .

Conversely, 'me' is mental energy, mind, manufactured, mania, miserable, materialistic, matter, melancholy, myth . . .

Getting Back on Track

After a busy week and a weekend of visitors and not much time to myself or time to meditate, walk, read, write or do yoga, I felt down, kind of lost, off track and not knowing how to get back on it. I realised that I could spend hours or days trying to figure it out and stay in this fug. Maybe I would get a sense of how I got so off track, even though I had been feeling so centred recently. Maybe I wouldn't. I realised there was an alternative. Instead, I could just come out of my head, back into the here and now. Be aware of where I am and how I am feeling. Just accept that. Then work with any of the building blocks that I know are part of the way I want to live my life: sit quietly and do nothing, read something, go for a walk, drink water, eat something healthy, write it out, do some yoga, meditate.

I don't need to KNOW what it is that has brought me to this unhappy, painful place, even if I could 'figure it out', which usually I don't anyway. Instead, I can let go of the need to know and just concentrate on recentring myself by doing some of these things that help me to do that. These things that recently have helped me live more often than not from a place of peace, stillness, equilibrium, gratitude, joy, and appreciation. Even when I've not been in that place, I've found it easier and easier to get back to it, when I've noticed that I've slipped out of it, and I'm caught up in head stuff.

Intentions

I feel like I'm drifting on the sea of life and not making any effort to steer the boat. I don't know if it's a biological thing, or if it's more a lack of confidence or sense of capability thing. I don't think it's depression, although I sometimes feel black. Mostly I feel OK mentally, and often lately I feel real happiness and peace. When this feeling comes over me though, I just can't be bothered applying myself to anything or psyching myself up for anything. I keep telling myself it's OK, and just to go with the flow of it, but I feel as though I am wasting my life when I feel this way.

So how do I square that with creating all that I want to create, as well as looking after myself and my family?

I think the key is in inspiration. I think I need to create a compelling meaning in what I do, to inspire me to get on with what I need to do. HOWEVER I'm feeling.

I can be aware of what is head stuff and what is heart stuff, and soul stuff, as I do whatever I'm doing. I can notice and recognise how aligned I am or not with what I want. I need to not make this all a mental concept though; as then it will be about being in the right place mentally to feel motivated and follow through on what I want to do. Then I'm just back into head stuff.

It has to come from my soul, my intention. It has to be about what I deeply want for my life; so that as I work at living from awareness, all that I want to align myself with is all there, and I am living from my soul.

Then, if I'm not feeling focused or motivated in my head, I don't need to try to think differently or work on motivating or persuading myself. I just need to come back to my soul, to a place of Being. Then I will instinctively know what I need to do.

I just come back to being over, and over, and over, every day, instead of trying to figure anything out. From there, I can just live my life. From this place, I don't need to know or understand 'things'. I just need to trust and Be. Just feel the peace and joy in that and keep putting one foot in front of the other.

I want to do things differently. I love my life, and all that I have in it, and I don't want to waste a second of it forgetting that.

It's my mission to learn to live in and from this place most of the time.

My Own Power

This morning as I was doing some yoga and really enjoying it, as I did the warrior pose, I could feel my power. I normally love that pose anyway because I feel strong when I do it, but it felt different today. It felt like I could feel the power of my soul and spirit in my whole body. It felt like who I'm seen as in the world didn't exist, it was just the pure spiritual being, and I felt like I was the lifeforce.

It felt fantastic, and it felt so right and real and true. It felt like with that power you could do anything. I want to nurture this connection to my authentic power. I feel fierce with life, and I feel fierce. It's such a good feeling. I want to help other people to feel this way too, to find this power within themselves. I know that it's available to every human being that wants to find it. I think the only factors affecting how easy or difficult it might be to access, are how disconnected someone is from it, and how much they can believe that it exists.

As well as feeling fierce and powerful, being in this place, I also feel vibrantly alive. I don't even really know what I mean by that, but I feel it strongly. It feels like this power is love, is passion, is life, pure lifeforce. It is the power of Being.

This is really who I am, not all the stuff in my head. As I stare ahead, I feel like I have never looked out of my eyes from this place, not with feeling so strong and powerful. I've only had glimpses before. Now it feels like I'm in that power. That I am that power. I want to build on this, nurture it, strengthen it.

* * *

It's a few days later but I am feeling that power again this morning. I realised that feeling this way gives me an attitude. One that is about saying NO to the head stuff – the conditioning, the chatter, the fears, repetitive thoughts, the criticisms and judgements of myself and others.

This power is the opposite of all that; it is love, passion, meaning, potential. It is the lifeforce coursing through me.

Marianne Williamson says: 'Our deepest fear is not that we are inadequate. Our deepest fear is that we are powerful beyond measure.'[21]

That is this power. I can feel it. I can also see that the more I nurture it and consciously connect to it, it will get stronger. I will use that power to change myself and create what I am supposed to in the world. I can sense that this power is good and is just looking for a creative outlet in the world.

---

21   Marianne Williamson, *A Return to Love* (HarperCollins, 1992)

I think when we feel a sense of our own power, we don't know what to do with it. We've never been taught what to do with it. It feels scary, so we anaesthetise the feeling with sugar, or alcohol, or distract ourselves from the feeling by concentrating on the contents of our minds. Alternatively, we let our ego take hold of that sense of power and go into self-aggrandisement. That's why I can't be in my power and in my head, I have to be in Being before I'm truly connected to my power, and to the power of the lifeforce, in a real way.

Chapter Ten

Inhabiting Being

Let us all be human BEINGS,
rather than human doings.
May we all experience lives we
don't need to escape from.

We're back where we started, at Being. I hope you can see the clear process for coming into Being, and that in learning to live from it, you can transform your experience of life. You come out of your head and into your heart. You cultivate awareness and acceptance – you wake up, and you let go. Then as you cultivate both a grateful heart, and the creative energy of your soul, you come to live in the reality of your authentic self, and all that your life can be. You come to know your own soul, you learn to recognise it's promptings. Then you create and communicate in the world from your soul.

You come to fully inhabit the spiritual being that you are.

You have reached your longed-for state of Being. You have discovered the ultimate hidden treasure. You get to enjoy the rewards of Being every day. Just keep doing what you're doing. You've found the path, you know the way, but you still need to consciously put one foot in front of the other along that path moment by moment, day by day. As you do, you get to rest in the knowledge that you will know the way forward from now on.

You do this with humility. Not entertaining the thought that coming to live more from Being makes you any better a human being than anyone else, or more 'evolved' spiritually. You grow, and this growth is a deepening and broadening of your experience of yourself, and of life. If you can live more from Being, with humility, you will begin to experience the grace that comes from a relationship with your soul, and with the lifeforce.

> In Being, grace assists you in all that
> you endeavour to create, and also brings you home,
> to yourself.

Continuity from Living from Being

For years I craved continuity in my life. I always felt defeated by my own ingrained negative behaviour patterns. They would be triggered, and destroy my best efforts to stay on track with, for instance, starting a new project, losing weight, getting fitter, establishing new routines, or becoming more positive, etc. Time and time again, I felt caught in Groundhog Day. Back at square one, with my best efforts seeming to have ended up counting for nothing. When eventually I'd dust myself off and feel ready to psych myself up to try again, with whatever aspects of my life were the focus at that time, my perspective would have changed to one where all wasn't lost. I'd realise that I had made some progress, even if it was three steps forward two steps back. I just needed to regroup and keep trying.

Still, though, I lacked a sense of continuity, it didn't feel like I was building on anything that I'd done before. It wasn't until way down the twisty, bumpy, long road that I began to realise the sense of continuity I craved wasn't going to come from 'getting it right' with any of these projects, goals, or routines. Not by succeeding at accomplishing whatever the goal at the time was. It could only come from an underlying sense of security, of feeling that fundamentally I was OK and that everything was OK. I began to realise that it could only come from feeling connected to who I truly am, to my soul, to Being. The more I recognised the spiritual being that I am and built ways to stay connected to Being into my day-to-day life, the more I could feel that sense of continuity building.

I began to feel that there was something solid and true, that was pure me, that I was making stronger with each effort that I made in developing my connection to it. Something that was affected by nothing in the outside world, only by how much I paid attention to it and nurtured it. The weird and wonderful thing though, is that once I realised that, and made building that *continuity of connection to Being* my focus, rather than the projects, goals, or new routines, I seemed to become better at following through on these things anyway! It all seemed to work together, and I think that's what it's supposed to do. That's the beauty of it. That's the magic of it. This is how you fulfil the promise of your unique potential as a human being.

Journal:
Being My Authentic Self

I'll finish this section with some of my more recent journal extracts, about my experiences of living in, and from, Being. These were where I got to after developing my connection to Being for a while, and learning to live in and from it more and more.

The Experience Deepens

In the past few days, I feel as though I've found a new depth to just Being. Rather than merely finding some peace and stillness within me, through quieting my mind, which still feels beneficial, I've been able to detach from my mind, however briefly. In doing so, I have felt an incredible calmness and peace come over me, almost as if the world pauses, or slows down. Then this sense of a pure and complete peace descends on me. Well, it really feels like I become it.

When this happens, I feel like I am hyper-aware of the present moment and everything it contains, and all of my senses are alert, but in a very relaxed, not tense, way. Everything feels so right and so true in this space, it feels like I have a knowing that this is who I truly am, without any doubt, who we all are, and it is where we are all meant to live our lives from. I realise it's not something I can hold onto or force. It feels that all I can do is remember about it.

I get a weird sensation that my body is something I occupy, almost like it's a shell that I just inhabit. That feels strange.

Knowing

I really felt today how much I am ready to make my primary focus Being rather than doing. It seems so clear to me that Being (being: present, aware, in my heart) is how we as human beings are supposed to live, regardless of what we 'do' in the world. In doing so, we become who we truly are and realise our ultimate potential.

It feels like a calm acceptance, a knowing. I also see my mental concepts for what they are. Most of the things I'm thinking don't matter; the thoughts are white noise. When I can reside in Being, I notice my mind jumping from thought to thought, latching onto some intensely, and being drawn into getting totally absorbed in them. The trick is to stay in Being while doing, and remember to notice my thoughts rather than thinking them and becoming totally absorbed in them, and therefore cut off from Being.

I noticed today how much my mind is always seeking something to latch onto, never satisfied. The thing that will satisfy, distract, amuse, excite, reassure, pacify, or anaesthetise . . . I could see the futility of it, the insanity of it, and how much it detracts from what is real, now, the present, and all that it contains – the world in every moment.

My soul is limitless, through its connection to the lifeforce – when I'm in Being.

Continuity

It struck me powerfully this morning that the feeling of continuity which I strive for comes from consistently making the time to turn my attention towards the spiritual being that I am, to my soul.

I had thought that the continuity was about the consistency of doing the whole package of things that make up how I want to live my life: eating healthily, meditation, walking, family time, etc. I realise now though, it's much more about making time and space for the spiritual that gives me that feeling of continuity, of forward progress, of growth, of creating something. It also gives me a sense of knowing who I am. I think there is a thread of purpose and meaning that runs through any time and space that I make for the spiritual. For coming into Being. That is the continuity that I've been craving.

Clarity

I have just returned from a two-hour walk to the lighthouse on Holy Isle. I felt the wind on my face and could hear the ocean breaking on the pebbly shore, but my mind felt manic – an array of intense thoughts. I kept trying to come back to my surroundings, but my mind was in overdrive.

When I got to the lighthouse, I sat on a ledge of grass at the top of the cliff, on the peninsula, looking over the sea. I felt vulnerable sitting there in the strong wind, but it also felt exhilarating. No thoughts, just calm, peace, and connection to my soul and to the lifeforce, to something. A knowing.

A knowing with utter certainty, and absolute clarity, that being in this place of connection within myself – Being – was the ultimate goal of my endeavours in life. Although I've known that before and understood it, this felt like knowing it in a deeper, more visceral, real way. My mind was stilled, and the deep peace felt wonderful and beautiful. It might have lasted two minutes or ten, I don't know, but it doesn't matter.

On my walk back, my mind started jabbering away again, but I felt calmer and more satisfied. Even now, a couple of hours later, the memory of the feeling of deep peace feels very vivid, in my body, not my mind. It is as though it has left an imprint inside me, and because of that, it feels easier to find that place within me. I feel really thankful for my life. I know now that I don't need to figure anything out, or read anything in particular, or talk to myself internally, or wrestle with things . . . I just need to remember. This place is always there within me. That I can go to it anytime. That I will find peace and happiness there.

Epilogue

In Being I find the still, calm place within me, then I remember that this IS me. I look out to the world from this place and know that, in this moment, everything is OK. I look within, and know that, in this moment, I am OK.

Learning to live in, and from, Being is not a destination, it is a way of life. It is not a magic wand, it is a pointer. It is not a set of rails that keep you on track, it is a set of signposts that can show you the way back, whenever you stumble.

I hope that by coming to understand the process I've shared in this book it will inspire you to begin your own journey into Being.

It feels great when you start experiencing elements of your vision, and well worth the effort, but it also feels great, long before that, when you first know that from becoming more aware, you are accessing the place of Being within yourself. Even from that very first simple step, you start to understand that by cultivating residing in Being, for *any* amount of time, you are connecting with your true self, and experiencing life *exactly* as you are meant to. If you only do this, in every moment that you do, you are fulfilling your human potential, and coming to know your own soul. The rewards of doing all this far outweigh the time, effort, and energy you have to put into achieving it.

Keep coming back to this process over and over for the rest of your life. Master it, and enjoy it because a more real, authentic experience of life comes from engaging with life as your true self.

Nobody's life is perfect; mine certainly isn't. Life is often difficult. You'll have all the usual struggles and juggles that come with being a human being in this world in which we live. You may also have some of your own unique ones. However, when you shuffle off this mortal coil, if the least you have done is really come into your Being, know your own soul, and experienced living as your authentic self, you will have achieved far more than most other human beings ever do. You'll have fulfilled the promise of your unique potential as a human being.

Acknowledgements

I know it's a cliché, but I don't care – this book has been a labour of love. I have put my heart and soul into it, over several years. It would just have stayed as my accumulated writing if I hadn't had the good fortune to be able to work with the team of people that helped me put it out into the world.

First, thank you to Sandy Draper, a wonderful editor and a joy to work with. I hope this is only the first of many books that you help me birth. Heather Macpherson at Raspberry Creative Type, thank you for generously enduring my perfectionistic tendencies when it came to the aesthetics of typesetting and cover design. I hope you agree it was worth it! Sue Juby, thank you for your keen eye for detail in the proofreading. Thanks also to Mary Turner Thomson of WhiteWater Publishing for always being on hand for publishing-related advice, and a laugh.

Throughout my journey, as I've lived the experiences detailed in this book, and many, many more, my friend Louise Welsh has witnessed both the rollercoaster and the calmer waters. She has been hearing about my journey into Being for years, and years, and gave me detailed, honest feedback on the manuscript of this book as it developed. Thank you. I'm so grateful for your friendship and writing support. Also, my scriptwriter friend Ros Borland has been a great cheerleader and support on my writing adventure. Thank you.

Finally, thank you to all my family for being so supportive of all my endeavours over the years; I really appreciate it. And an especially huge thanks for everything, and for putting up with me in general, to Annie, Chris, and Jack.

Further Reading

These are the books, out of the hundreds that I've devoured over the years, that stick out in my mind as being an integral part of my journey to Being. I've returned to many of them again and again and I hope they may prove useful to you too.

Ban Breathnach, Sarah, *Simple Abundance* (Warner Books USA, 1995)

Cameron, Julia, *The Artist's Way* (Tarcher, 1992)

Csikszentmihalyi, Mihaly, *Flow: The Psychology of Happiness* (Harper Perennial Modern Classics, 2008)

Dalai Lama, H.H. and Cutler, Howard C., *The Art of Happiness* (Hodder & Stoughton, 2011)

De Mello, Anthony, *Awareness* (Fount, 1997)

Doyle, Glennon, *Carry on Warrior* (Penguin, 2013)

_____, *Untamed* (Random House, 2020)

Frankl, Victor, *Man's Search for Meaning* (Rider, 2004)

Gilbert, Elizabeth, *Big Magic* (Bloomsbury Paperbacks, 2016)

_____, *Eat Pray Love* (Bloomsbury Paperbacks, 2009)

Goddard, Neville, *The Power of Awareness* (G. & J. Publishing Co., 1952)

Gunaratana, Bhante, Mindfulness in Plain English (Wisdom Publications, 2015)

Jeffers, Susan, *Feel the Fear and Do It Anyway* (Arrow Books, 1991)

Milner, Marion, *A Life of One's Own* (Routledge, 2011)

Moorjani, Anita, *Dying to Be Me* (Hay House, 2012)

Parke, Simon, *One Minute Mindfulness* (Hay House UK, 2014)

Peck, Scott M., *The Road Less Travelled* (Arrow, 1990)

Rogers, Carl R., *A Way of Being* (Houghton Mifflin, 1992)

Singer, Michael A., *The Untethered Soul* (New Harbinger Publications, 2007)

Strayed, Cheryl, *Wild* (Atlantic Books, 2015)

Tolle, Eckhart, *A New Earth* (Dutton, 2005)

_____, *Stillness Speaks* (Hodder & Stoughton, 2011)

_____, *The Power of Now* (Hodder & Stoughton, 2001)

Williamson, Marianne, *A Return to Love* (HarperCollins, 1992)

Winfrey, Oprah, *The Wisdom of Sundays* (Macmillan, 2017)

Zukav, Gary, *The Seat of the Soul* (Ebury, 1991)

About the Author

I thought it would paint a truer, more meaningful picture for you and put this book in context, if I told you the significant things that I've *experienced* in my life, rather than give you my CV! These are the things that have shaped my world and me. This is my autobiography in six paragraphs.

I had a reasonably happy childhood in a loving, supportive family, although I was also bullied badly for a while in primary school. Mostly I remember always feeling like I didn't fit in somehow, that the other children didn't like me, that I was different, or wrong, in some way. Thankfully, I experienced making real friends for the first time in my teens, with whom I'm blessed to still be friends with now, decades later – Helen, Jackie, and Maureen.

I developed bulimia in my late teens into my twenties. Eventually, becoming pregnant was the catalyst that finally made me determined to knock it on the head. Going forwards, though, I still used food and alcohol as physical escape routes in trying to manage my psychological, emotional, and spiritual struggles. Due to that, I've been overweight, several times, but have also experienced having a lean, strong, healthy body. I've also had regular, debilitating migraines since my teens.

I've experienced feelings of depression and anxiety to varying degrees at various times in my life. At times feeling lost, alone, completely inadequate, full of self-doubt, as well as experiencing vicious self-loathing and self-hatred. Yet, I managed to hide most of this behind a super-confident, friendly, cheerful public persona. To compensate, I needed to have regular times of solitude, to retreat inside myself, to regroup.

I've experienced over twenty career paths from barmaid, fitness instructor, through admin assistant, researcher and director in television, counsellor/therapist, to businesswoman. On each of these paths, I've learned different things about myself and about life Likewise, travelling around the world for months myself in my twenties, changed my perspective on myself and my life..

I've had myriad experiences of being a mother of two children, a wife, a sister, a daughter, and a friend. Relationships have always been important to me. However much I've struggled and wanted to retreat from the world, I've always made an effort to try to keep the lines of communication and connection going and prioritise my relationships.

What I experience more often these days is all that living in, and from, Being brings, which feels amazing. As well as writing, I'm involved in running an artisan food production business, I volunteer with a homeless charity, and spend time with the people I love, as much as possible. I write, I walk, I read, do yoga (badly), and meditate. I love my life (mostly!).

Connect with me:
www.lynnbmann.com
Twitter: @LynnBMann1 and/or @BEING_LBM
Facebook: Lynn B. Mann and/or BEING
Instagram: lynnb.mann and/or beinglbm

Reviews

If you've enjoyed this book, I'd greatly appreciate you posting a review online please, either wherever you bought it, or on it's page on Amazon – you can now do this as long as you have an Amazon account, even if you didn't buy the book there. It really does help other readers in deciding if it might be helpful/suitable for them.

Thank you so much in advance if you do.

Other Books
by Lynn B. Mann

Being 21

Towards greater self-understanding in 21 questions

(Being Books, 2020)

HBK ISBN: 978-1-8381628-0-1
PBK ISBN: 978-1-8381628-1-8

'Who am I really?'

What 21-year-old doesn't ask themself this question. Entering your twenties, turning 21, and the next few years, is an intense time in our lives. Supposedly it's when we become an adult. Where we begin to map out what our life might look like. When we're likely to have lots of big decisions to make around careers, studying, where we'll live, and in relationships. How are we meant to navigate all of this, if we don't really know who we are or what we want?

Being 21 is a beautiful book on the outside and meaningful within. This original and attractive 21st birthday gift introduces a process of self-questioning, which helps build confidence, and capability. It also supports mental and emotional wellbeing.

Throughout the process, the reader is helped in developing more: confidence, self-esteem, resilience, courage, adaptability, self-trust, and determination.

In 21 carefully crafted, powerful questions, former counsellor/therapist Lynn B. Mann has created a step-by-step guide towards the reader knowing more who they are, and what they want their life to be about.